HOW TO ENJOY RETIREMENT

In this Series

How to Choose a Private School
How to Claim State Benefits
How to Enjoy Retirement
How to Get a Job Abroad
How to Get That Job
How to Help Your Child at School
How to Keep Business Accounts
How to Live & Work in America
How to Live & Work in Australia
How to Pass Exams Without Anxiety
How to Raise Business Finance
How to Run a Club or Society
How to Speak Well in Public
How to Survive at College
How to Use a Library
How to Write That Book

other titles inpreparation

How To Books General Editor Roland Seymour

ENJOY RETIREMENT
A Handbook of Opportunities

Harry Gray

Northcote House

First published in 1987 by Northcote House Publishers Ltd,
Harper & Row House, Estover Road, Plymouth PL6 7PZ, United Kingdom.
Tel: Plymouth (0752) 705251. Telex: 45635. Fax: (0752) 777603.

British Library Cataloguing in Publication Data
Gray, Harry
  How to enjoy retirement: a handbook of
  opportunities. — (How to series).
  1. Retirement — Great Britain
  I. Title
  646.7′9   HQ1064.Gt

ISBN 0-7463-0323-8

Printed and bound in Great Britain

Contents

Introduction

More people are retiring from full-time employment today than ever before and the proportion of retired people in the population looks like increasing indefinitely. One reason is that people are retiring earlier — some in their early fifties and many before the traditional retiring ages of 60 (for women) and 65 (for men). Some people now will spend more years in retirement than they did in full-time work. Some very lucky people will have nearly half a century of retirement to enjoy. Indeed, retirement is something to look forward to positively, and your retirement years should be the best years of your life.

The best way to get the most out of retirement is to retire as early as you can — but you don't *have* to stop working. Indeed, one of the big mistakes about retirement is to think that it means no longer working. You no longer need to earn your weekly crust, but you can certainly still be gainfully and satisfyingly engaged in work that *you* now choose to do.

Many people change gear in their work in their late forties and take on different responsibilities. They may slow down or have more responsibility, but also discover more freedom to make decisions; they will have earned the respect of their colleagues so that their judgment and opinions are valued. Retirement, at any age, is really an extension of that kind of job change. It is a time when, perhaps at last, you can take full charge of your own life for the whole of the day and do only those things that satisfy *you* without being beholden to anyone else.

The two key factors in retirement are that you no longer need to earn your basic living by — in most cases — having to work for someone else, and that you are free to decide how you occupy your time. People often spend their whole working life looking forward to retirement like this, but when it finally comes they find it hard to deal with, and become bored and unmotivated. Men suffer more from boredom in retirement than women; many do not enjoy as many years of retirement as they might, simply because they find transition from work to retirement too sudden and complete, leaving them at a loss as to what to do.

This book has been written to suggest a *positive* approach to retirement, and the many new opportunities it offers today for men and women, singles and couples. Let retirement mark the start of the fullest and happiest years of *your* life!

1
Retirement — Open Door of Opportunity

Most people approaching retirement cannot wait for the time of freedom from enforced work to come. Since the opportunity for retirement comes to nearly everyone sooner or later, it is good to look forward to it positively and prepare for it actively so that when it does come it can be an open door of opportunity.

- To *expect* a long and happy retirement is the surest way to make it such. To *dread* it as a misfortune is to guarantee a wasted and disappointing experience.

The best thing is to start preparing seriously about five years before the time comes. However, even if the decision is quite a sudden one, there is a lot that can be done in just a few weeks to prepare for the most exciting time of your life.

How about making a list of the things you are most looking forward to in retirement? To start you off some ideas are given on the following page. Against each item consider how you hope to achieve it. As you look back over your list you will realise how full and satisfying retirement can be.

Pre-retirement courses

Many companies offer pre-retirement courses to employees in their last year or two, and it's worth finding out if your own employer does this. Some companies send older employees on pre-retirement courses run by other organisations and pay the full cost. In some cases, a company will make provision for a reduced workload and lessened responsibilities for senior staff, to let them orientate themselves towards a new style of life. Large companies with redundancy schemes may allow up to a year or even two for staff to look for alternative employment or other ways of using their time in early retirement.

Objective	How to be achieved
1. Spend more time with the family	_____
2. Allow more time for friends and neighbours	_____
3. Take part in local community life	_____
4. Take a long holiday	_____
5. Sports and recreation	_____
6. Household jobs and improvements	_____
7. Gardening	_____
8. Clubs and organisations	_____
9. Have a good rethink about the future	_____
10. Move into a new house or flat	_____
11. Go abroad	_____
12. Start work on a pet project	_____
13. Get really fit	_____
14. Take part in church and social life	_____
15. Help others	_____
16. Visit distant friends and/or relatives	_____
17. Write letters, articles or even a book	_____
18. Move to a new town or area	_____
19. Renew subscription(s)	_____
20. Change the car	_____
21. Explore the sales or local auctions	_____
22. Develop a new business idea	_____
23. Get an overdue medical and/or dental check-up	_____
24. Accept a long-standing invitation	_____
25. Fulfil a long-standing obligation	_____
26. Explore the local reference library	_____
27. Join a committee	_____
28. Join a political party	_____
29. Turn some acquaintances into friends	_____

What **active steps** are you taking to prepare yourself for retirement? List the five most supportive actions you plan to take. To start you off, here are some suggestions:

What to do	How to do it
1. Reorganise personal finances — check mortgage, pension(s), insurance(s)	See accountant, bank manager, financial consultant
2. Plan future activities	Talk with family and friends
3. Collect information to help major decisions	Join pre-retirement association; use the addresses in this book
4. Join club or organisation	Visit Citizens' Advice Bureau; enquire at local library
5. Look for part-time work	Visit Job Centre or Employment Agency
6.	....
7.	....
8.	....
9.	....
10.	....

What else might you do to help prepare for your new life?

Whatever the circumstances of retirement, it pays to look upon your new state of life as something that should be enjoyable, fruitful, rewarding and immensely satisfying. If there is no provision for pre-retirement courses at work, then there will probably be some organised by the local **Adult Education** service (telephone the local **Education Office** or your local **College of Further Education**). Some newspapers and magazines organise such events and attendance may be free to readers.

● **Planning** for retirement is the surest way of managing this major life transition effectively and for the best personal benefit.

Men retiring

Men often experience more problems in facing retirement than women. This has to do with our social expectations of what is right for men and what is right for women. Men often invest all their energies in their job and their social life revolves around the company of other men. Much of what they do is competitive and concerned with personal achievement.

Some men secretly fear retirement and try to postpone it, snatching an extra year (or even months) or trying to extend their working life by going back part time. When they retire many men hardly know what to do with their time; there is no competitive structure for them to lock onto, and they are unused to such great expanses of leisure. They may have been looking forward to more time for 'hobbies' but find that life becomes boring because there is nothing to contrast their hobby with; it is no longer a foil to working for someone else.

●   Retirement is the time when you have **most personal choices.** You can at last take full charge of your own life.

Retirement creates an opportunity to embark upon an entirely new lifestyle, with a balance of interesting and varied activities. The easiest way of starting this new life is to take on specific domestic responsibilities so that life at home is equally shared with one's partner. Shopping can be a shared activity rather than the sole responsibility of one.

●   **What main activities** do you want most to enjoy when you have retired? Decide on two or three important ones and plan how you are going to become involved in them. What things could hold you back? How will you deal with them?

Women retiring

A large number of women live longer than men, so their retirement generally lasts longer. No one really understands why women should outlive men; one factor may be that women's lives do not change so dramatically when they retire. Of course, women can retire five years earlier than men which may help, too, but they also continue, in most marriages, to be responsible for domestic work. Most women think of themselves as doing two jobs, one looking after the home, the other going out to work.

●   **Married women** can start on a totally new life when their husbands retire. The new life is just as much an opportunity for both partners as it is for one.

"Darling, will you marry me for the next
40 years as well?"

In retirement, the basic **domestic lifestyle** is fundamental. Women who have gone out to work understand the need for proper domestic arrangements and simply continue to do the basic things needed to allow home to be supported. Perhaps women are also more used to catering for other people and their needs as well as their own. Men tend to be rather selfish in many conventional marriages; could it be that altruism is one of the strongest factors in maintaining good health and a positive attitude to life?

Are you planning any changes in your domestic role on retirement? Consider the list below:

1. Running the house, domestic chores, etc
2. Shopping and budgeting
3. Gardening
4. Decorating and improvements
5. Cooking and entertaining
6. Deciding on evenings out or weekends away
7. More shared plans and pleasures
8. Taking more part in local life
9. ....
10. ....
11. ....
12. ....
13. ....
14. ....

Men and women together

Most people begin retirement as partners and it is important to develop as true *working* partners. People who have been in business together often understand the nature of a real working partnership and can continue this into their retired life together. But most couples will have to work at it and discover a way of sharing responsibility and support if they are to get along well together. The truth is that for many people the worst aspect of retirement is that married partners have to spend so long together. Husbands get under their wife's feet and wives expect their husbands to run around after them all the time. Both now need to re-examine the marriage contract taken for granted for so many years.

● Retirement requires a new form of **contract between domestic partners** that needs to be well understood by both partners if the coming years are to be harmonious.

Well before the *first* partner retires, some time must be spent together looking at what each expects of the other. How will these expectations continue into retirement? Try making a list of what each requires of the other and work through it, talking over what is still acceptable and what will have to be changed.

Questionnaire
Our strengths and weaknesses in retirement
Just tick the statements which you think most apply:

	Me	Partner
Positive about the future		
Rather uncertain about the future		
Willing to adapt		
Hard to break old habits		
Can live more economically		
Find it hard to cut down on spending		
Outgoing and sociable		
Not able to make friends easily		
Healthy and fit		
Worried about health		
Plenty of accessible family		
Few family members close at hand		
Plenty of friends		
Few friends		
Lots of plans and ideas		
Find filling in the time difficult		
Feel secure in marriage		
Find close relationships a strain		
Have mutuality of interests		
Pursue individual interests		
Enjoy each other's friends		
Have own friends		
Enjoy each other's families		
Not close to in-laws		
Willing to give in to the other		
Busy with own concerns		
Willing to move		
Not happy about moving		

Now try adding to the list, considering only *positive* things:

Strengths in retirement

Mine	My partner's
....	....
....	....
....	....
....	....
....	....
....	....
....	....

LIFESTYLE

Not many people think of their lives as having a particular **'lifestyle'**. Yet we all have a way of living that is unique to us, and have things in common with other people, particularly our friends. We can recognise this, for example, in people who are dedicated churchgoers; there are certain things they do and certain things they do not do that characterise their whole lives. Often it is someone else who recognises the individual's lifestyle — the individual concerned just takes it all for granted. It is worth clarifying what our own lifestyle is, because the **quality** of our retirement will largely depend on the continued fulfilment of the needs our lifestyle serves to supply.

Looking at your lifestyle

● A good way of looking at our lifestyle is to list the things we do that we feel we could not do without, then the ones which hardly matter to us. Then, by the side of each, we can record how often each has arisen during the last week. An example is given below. From this exercise we can discover whether what we *believe* we need is important to us, or not. It's a simple assessment of what must happen in our retired life if we are to remain happy and contented.

Matter	Has arisen	Doesn't matter	Has arisen
Visitors	None	Theatre visits	Twice
Library visits	Six	Train trips	Never
Radio	All the time	Supermarket visits	Once

Laid back or active

Another aspect of lifestyle is whether we are easy going and laid back, or busy and active. Once we have embarked on our retirement, it will be hard to change our natural pace. On the whole, people take it easier in retirement; for example no early buses to catch or city traffic jams to avoid. But we all have different emotional patterns to our day and week. Some of us are morning people and early risers; others don't really come round until late morning and are most active after eight o'clock at night. Since for most of us the need to work has been paramount, we may feel ridiculously guilty that we adopt in retirement a quite different pattern of life. Of course, there will never be the same constant pressure on us that there was at work, but some people feel uncomfortable without pressure while others are glad to be free of it. If we do need pressures we can create them for ourselves, so that *we* control them instead of someone else; and if we don't need them we can make sure they don't reappear.

Changing attitudes

It is generally thought that we become more liberal and open-minded as we grow older. This may not be true — some people clearly become more restricted in outlook and less tolerant — but a happy disposition usually has plenty of tolerance and understanding. Older people who have become embittered and intolerant — especially of young people — are likely to put themselves under increasing strain. In retirement one's own attitudes generally need to become more relaxed, understanding, and tolerant — though, of course, we don't want to give up our values and standards. Indeed, the very fact of being more relaxed should help us encourage others to higher standards of performance, since we are not threatening them in the way that busy people often do.

Your tolerance rating

To find your 'tolerance rating' score yourself from 0 to 3 for each item below.

- 3 *more* tolerant than most
- 2 *as* tolerant as most people
- 1 *less* tolerant than the average person

When you have done the exercise get your partner to do it *for* you and compare the differences. They *might* see you rather differently!

Check your tolerance rating

I am more/as/less tolerant than others of:

_____	noisy neighbours	_____	sport
_____	the younger generation	_____	old people
_____	inlaws	_____	traffic jams
_____	people with money to burn	_____	air travel
_____	people with very little money in retirement	_____	late trains
		_____	political demonstrations
_____	television	_____	traffic wardens
_____	cats and dogs	_____	council officials
_____	different religions	_____	one-parent families
_____	other peoples' opinions	_____	the unemployed
_____	jazz	_____	Inspectors of Taxes
_____	pop music	_____	the British winter
_____	Radio 3	_____	foreign food

How did you rate?

The maximum score is 75. The higher the score the more tolerant you are.

70-75   You can't be living in this world!
60-69   Perhaps you don't go out much!
50-59   You are pretty laid back.
40-49   At least *something* annoys you.
30-39   Do you tend to be opinionated?
20-29   You must get a lot of people's backs up.
10-19   You must be impossible to live with!
 0- 9   You didn't do the exercise. What's bugging you?

Consider the matters about which you were most *intolerant*. Which would you like to change? How could you go about it?

Subject	How I can change
. . . .	. . . .
. . . .	. . . .
. . . .	. . . .
. . . .	. . . .
. . . .	. . . .
. . . .	. . . .
. . . .	. . . .
. . . .	. . . .

We need to remember that our attitudes towards other people reflect our attitudes to ourselves. If we are over-critical and unreasonably demanding, we may not in reality be entirely satisfied with ourselves. We need to be more relaxed, more accepting of ourselves. The way to do this is by thinking the best of ourselves, enjoy being the sort of person we are. None of us is perfect, but it is our very imperfections that make us interesting and endear us to our friends. If we begin to think well of ourselves we respond accordingly and turn out to be nicer than we thought. We soon begin to think well of others, and that is part of the secret of happiness.

Here is another little idea. Jot down all the things you *like* about yourself and all the things you *don't like*. By the side of the things you like, say how you are going to maintain them. By the side of the things you don't like write how you are going to change them. Here is an example:

Things I like about me:	And after retirement
I have a happy disposition	Share happiness with others
I dress well	Look smart when shopping
. . . .	. . . .
. . . .	. . . .
. . . .	. . . .

Things I don't like about me	And after retirement
I am fat	Eat healthier food, take exercise
Don't make friends easily	Speak to someone new every day
. . . .	. . . .
. . . .	. . . .
. . . .	. . . .
. . . .	. . . .

MAKING A NEW START

It's usually best to make a gradual transition from working life to retirement, though there is a point when we are aware that retirement is inevitable. It's rather like deciding whether to go on holiday; once you have decided where you want to go, you go to the travel agent and book, and from then on it's a countdown to the first day. The better you prepare yourself — in whatever way is most appropriate to you — the better you will enjoy the holiday; it won't take long then to relax when away from home. Retirement is one long super holiday.

● Retirement is the **best opportunity** you have ever had to make a fresh start and to prepare for the best time ever.

There are several areas in which you can begin to prepare yourself — personally, in your family relationships, with regard to work, and in opportunities to travel. All of these will be explored in greater detail later, but let's take a first look at them.

Personal considerations

The most important personal consideration is the acceptance of retirement as a **positive stage** of development in life. Sadly, for some people, the whole idea of retirement is unacceptable. They are attached not only to their work but to the kind of family and domestic relationship which being a wage earner often entails. But retirement needn't be the end of work; as we shall see later there is plenty of work to be done — sometimes a good deal more than when employed.

For many people their sense of identity comes from being employed and being separated economically from the home. It is being away from home each day, and being important to someone else, that matters. Being relegated to the chimney corner seems to involve a loss of dignity. Perhaps we think of retired people as being in some way 'rejects', as no longer useful and so of lower standing than people still working. But this cannot be true since everyone retires some time, and having worked and been self-supporting is a major achievement.

● Being retired is **having arrived.**

Perhaps what is more privately worrying in retirement is having to accept more responsibility for oneself. No longer will there be anyone above you to measure your effort, reward you, and decide your routines. In retirement it's very much up to you. All this ought to be welcomed — it is a better measure of your skills and abilities that you are responsible for yourself and have to evaluate your own progress.

Being fully responsible for oneself is a measure of **maturity**; retirement is both a test of maturity and an opportunity for it to be freely exercised. You are no longer anyone else's person but your own — perhaps for the first time in your life.

Family considerations

But the freedom to be yourself has natural restraints. Indeed, there is no freedom without restraint of some sort. For most of us there are family considerations which matter a good deal to us. Retired people often see their new-found leisure as an opportunity to see more of the family, especially if they live a long way from home. They may start visiting them and staying for long periods. Such visits are usually very welcome but there is also a risk. Grown-up children invariably live different kinds of lives from their parents and don't really appreciate *too* long a stay from their parents.

Instead of making their own lives fuller, perhaps parents use their children as a substitute. This frequently happens when a widow or widower moves to live with one of their children. The trouble is that, with the best will in the world, parents can become a nuisance. The best advice is to leave children very much to their own lives while you get on with your own.

"Is there anything I can do for you now I am at home?"

Most retired people will have a spouse or companion at home and in some cases a grown up but unmarried son or daughter. The previously working father and/or mother needs to establish a new relationship with the 'family' that will be creative and fulfilling to everyone. It is no use staying at home and becoming more and more dependent on those whose life continues much as before. Being retired means making positive and new contributions to everyone's happiness. A good way to start is to ask everyone for one thing they would like you to do for them now you have more time on your hands — and then to *do* it.

Some retired couples look forward to an idyllic companionship in their 'declining years' but this is usually a great mistake. Darby and Joan existences are not usually well adapted to retirement even though couples grow closer together.

● Retirement is a time to **expand one's friendships,** not restrict them.

Even making up a regular foursome with the same couple is not always to be advised; there is usually plenty of room for people in one's life and one can always use the family to make friends across the generations.

Work

Just because you have finished your lifetime's employment, it doesn't mean that there is no more work left to be done. Going back to the same employment part-time is not a good idea for most people; your part-time presence only underlines the fact that you have retired. But you might want to do similar work elsewhere — so long as it is part-time.

Many retired people like to take on a part-time job which is quite unlike anything they have done before and often they enjoy a job that previously they would have considered too menial. Just as students learn about the democracy of work in vacation jobs, so older people can discover that all work has dignity by doing jobs they might have considered beneath them. There are a lot of part-time jobs that suit retired people very well and provide them with more satisfaction than they may have had in a highly-paid but routine and mundane job in full employment.

Some part-time jobs that retired people have taken include office or school maintenance and cleaning, night-watching, baby-sitting, caring for invalids, book-keeping, helping with a shop or market stall, gardening. None has a particularly high social status but they can be rewarding and interesting.

Interests

Leisure interests are likely to be more varied and have more time devoted to them in retirement than before. Some people look forward to unlimited time to indulge in their favourite pastime, and why not? — fishing, painting, photography, walking, gardening, collecting can be lifelong interests.

But some activities are not really suitable for unlimited leisure even if they seem to be at first glance. Certainly one cannot play squash or golf all day long or even every day.

● **List your leisure interests** and evaluate them for variety overall. Do you have a good 'balance'? The list has been started off for you.

Interest	Sedentary	Out of doors	Active	Mentally rewarding	Emotionally rewarding
reading	√			√	√
walking		√	√		√
cooking			√		√
cycling		√	√		√
dramatics			√	√	√
TV	√			√	

- The secret is to have a lot of **varied interests** which involve meeting lots of different people rather than a solitary interest in which companions are few. It is easy to become wrapped up in oneself; one needs to keep the windows on the world ever open.

Travel

Not everyone wants to travel. Some people have done enough travelling to last them a lifetime, but for many people retirement is a time when opportunity for travel becomes more frequent and accessible. For one thing, one can travel at times when prices are reduced and stay for longer periods than during employment. One of the ways of keeping mentally alert is to use travel to develop one's interests purposefully rather than just for taking 'holiday' trips. Opportunities for travel can be exploited in all sorts of ways to provide an added dimension to life not usually possible before. For instance, acting as a business courier is a possibility while running messages for local businesses is another.

Where to live

A frequent topic of consideration is whether to **move away** to another area on retirement. At one time this was quite common. Indeed, some parts of the country have been nicknamed 'costa geriatrica' because of all the old people living there. Unless there are very good reasons for moving, such as health or inheritance, it is probably best not to move. One's friends will tend to be where one has lived for a long time and making new friends of the right kind is difficult after retirement ('there are no friends like old friends') though one may make many acquaintances.

Costs of removal can be prohibitive and mistakes are too costly to rectify. If you must move, try to do so well ahead of actual retirement. It is perhaps unwise to move just to be nearer members of the family, especially one's children — *they* may have to move for job purposes and then you can be left alone. It is also wise not to go and live in the same house as one's children unless there are good medical reasons for so doing.

If you *do* contemplate moving far away, rather than just to a smaller and more manageable home in the area you have lived and worked in, great thought should be given to the idea. Here are some key considerations:

- improved environment
- more manageable house
- easier local travel
- closer to amenities
- cheaper to run

- nearer more 'like-minded' people
- better local travel facilities
- more accessible to friends
- . . . .
- . . . .

Clothes

Some people stockpile clothes before retirement with the idea of not having to buy many more. This is ridiculous because fashions change and giving up some fashion awareness is one of the ways of allowing retirement to become a period of personal decline. Self respect means that one goes on buying clothes as part of life. Of course, we all have old and favourite clothes but as our body changes shape (which it always does) they no longer suit us and cannot be worn all the time. Taking a lively interest in clothes is as important for men as women and is a means of keeping in touch with the contemporary world. Many people in retirement have more time for shopping for personal things — or can at least organise their time for shopping more conveniently.

New clothes do not have to be expensive and certainly one doesn't have to follow the fashions of the very young. There are always reasonably-priced clothes to be bought and always fashions that enhance our appearance consistent with our age. Dressing well in later life is a measure of maturity.

The single state

Although for most people, retirement will begin in the company of a spouse or companion, one will probably survive the other and it is quite unreasonable to assume that the situation at the beginning of retirement will not change. At some point you may have to continue retirement alone and it is then that some of the ideas mentioned will become important. You are looking to improve the quality of your independence, not dependence, as you grow older.

However an increasing number of people reach retirement as single persons and some will never have married even though they may have children. This is why belonging to a community of people of various ages is valuable, and most good neighbourhoods have this quality. Whatever you do, let it enrich the quality of self-reliance and resourcefulness. Retirement is the time to do all those things you have not had time to do and fulfil yourself in a rounded way so that you are not only good company for others but good company for yourself.

	Checklist
	Retirement — the open door of opportunity

☐ Preparing for retirement well in advance?
☐ List of things to look forward to?
☐ Investigate pre-retirement courses?
☐ Sharing of domestic matters with partner?
☐ Mutual understanding of strengths and weaknesses with partner?
☐ Re-appraisal of lifestyle and attitudes?
☐ Special family considerations?
☐ Plenty of work and leisure interests to follow?
☐ Checked the addresses/contacts at the back of this book?

it for income. The list is started off for you:

- jewellery ....
- pictures ....
- antique furniture ....
- antique china ....
- antique silver ....
- musical instruments ....
- boat ....
- land ....

begin retirement with meagre financial provision and have to find ways of augmenting their pension that almost means a continuation of working life.

● As you approach retirement, make a **financial audit** of your resources.

If you own your house it is likely to be your biggest financial asset. It is certainly worth finding out whether some of the capital wrapped up in it can be realised. For example, you may be able to live in a smaller house; selling the bigger house would provide you with some capital to invest as well as an easier home to run and finance. Or your house may be large enough to be converted into flats for sale or rent, or 'bed-sits' to ensure a regular income.

● It is worth looking closely at **other assets** whose value you may not realise.

Make a list of what you own that you think may have value and put a rough evaluation alongside. It is worth having certain objects **professionally valued** because you may be able to realise that value and invest

£
£
£
£
£
£
£
. . . . £
. . . . £
. . . . £
. . . . £
. . . . £
. . . . £
. . . . £
. . . . £
. . . . £
. . . . £
. . . . £
. . . . £
. . . . £

Managing money

There is always plenty of advice available on investment and savings but it usually costs money, however little.

● Financial advice is only as good as the person who *receives* it; we do not suddenly alter our ways on retirement!

The handling of money is a very personal matter and not always rational, so we need to understand just what *meaning* money has for us. We all manage our money differently and each of us would probably find anyone else's way to be troublesome or eccentric.

For example, one important question could be, should we use cash or credit cards as the normal way of spending money? Neither is necessarily better than the other. If you tend to spend the cash in your pocket or purse it may be better to have credit cards in reserve. But if you run up large accounts it may be better to experiment with spending only cash.

Write down the things you want to do for you in your retirement. Here are some examples:

☐   Get out of debt (e.g. paying off Hire Purchase)
☐   Buy a new outfit of clothes
☐   Go on a long holiday
☐   Help the children or grandchildren
☐   Change the car
☐   Move home
☐   Redecorate the house from top to bottom
☐   Start up a small business
☐   Buy an annuity
☐   Pay off the mortgage
☐   Install a new bathroom or kitchen
☐   Ensure a secure financial future
☐   Reduce the cost of existing borrowings or outgoings
☐   ....
☐   ....
☐   ....
☐   ....
☐   ....

Ask yourself:

●   What proportion of your income do you expect to allocate to each?
●   How do you intend to achieve this?

Fixed incomes

Are you on a truly **fixed income**? If so you will need to organise your spending very carefully and budget by the week, month and year. This means keeping within your budget and spreading your spending over fixed periods. Fixed incomes tend to decrease in value over time, due to both inflation and your own expanded needs. Human nature being what it is, we tend to increase the kinds of things we spend money on rather than reduce them. The interests of our friends can be a potent factor in increasing our spending because we are tempted to do the same sorts of things they do.

When you do budget on a fixed income, always leave something in **reserve** and put it somewhere that makes it difficult to get at. Remember that at some times of the year, such as Christmas and holidays, there are always additional costs and you are more likely to spend more than last time, not less. If you do spend less that is a true bonus.

On the next page you will find a simple Budget Sheet that you might find useful to start with in considering your new financial status.

	Before retiring	After retiring
Income		
Salary or wages	£	£
State Pension	£	£
Occupational Pension	£	£
Other Income (eg from investments)	£	£
Less Income Tax	(£)	(£)
Less National Insurance Contributions	(£)	(£)
Total Net Income:	£	£

	Before retiring	After retiring
Expenditure		
Mortgage or rent	£	£
Rates	£	£
Food	£	£
Clothes	£	£
House repairs/maintenance	£	£
Decorating	£	£
Telephone	£	£
Insurances	£	£
Car expenses	£	£
Travel (fares)	£	£
Pension (if continuing contributions)	£	£
Life assurance	£	£
Holidays	£	£
Other	£	£
....	£	£
....	£	£
....	£	£
....	£	£
....	£	£
....	£	£
....	£	£
....	£	£
Total Expenditure	£	£

Income less spending

Here are some of the expenses that may **increase** when you retire. They need to be budgeted ahead of retirement:

- Extra heating/lighting bills
- Extra spending on entertainment and hobbies
- Replacement of company car
- Private health insurance
- Replacement for 'perks' in job (fares, lunches, discounts)
- Extra cost of additional activities (eg more frequent shopping, correspondence)

"I've still got a few luncheon vouchers left over."

Saving

Whatever your income, and wherever it comes from, try to save a little each week. Saving is a basic attitude of mind and is a key to good money management. If you find it difficult to save for the sake of saving, then save for specific purchases. These purchases may be luxuries or near-necessities. Shoes or an article of clothing may suddenly need replacing — not just because they are worn but because you really don't feel right in them. If you have £50 put away for such a purpose then the spending becomes a pleasure rather than an anxiety.

- Money is something to be enjoyed and to have control over. Saving is a way of increasing your enjoyment because it provides you with freedom of choice.

☐   For medical emergencies
☐   To maintain an older-style property
☐   To help the children or grandchildren
☐   For a really good holiday
☐   For a major expense
☐   For a rainy day
☐   ....
☐   ....
☐   ....
☐   ....
☐   ....
☐   ....
☐   ....
☐   ....

A number of **regular bills** can be saved for by the use of stamps or through instalments. Gas, electricity, telephone and television can be catered for in this way. But buying on credit, as with catalogue purchases, is a bad way of paying by instalments because you may come to resent going on paying for something you already have and you may well end up paying more than in the local high street.

Changing your ways
On the whole, people do not automatically change their ways with money just because they are retired; everyone has to **make some adjustments.**

- Try drawing up a list of all the ways you spend money and evaluate them to see if they are the best way.
- Try to change the ways you least approve of and enjoy the ones you feel most comfortable with.

For instance, any form of **gambling** is undesirable for anyone who does not have a good deal of surplus cash, but if you *do* gamble you should include the amounts in your budget and never exceed them. Some forms of gambling are more pleasurable than others and it may be worth changing to those ways that give most pleasure at least cost.

Another adjustment might involve when you withdraw cash. Some people draw money from the bank once a week. Some once a month and some whenever they feel they need it. Look carefully at this to see whether another method would cost you less in the long run. If you tend to spend whatever is in your pocket you should draw out at specific times and in specific amounts, but if you like to keep a good sum in your purse and hate to see it drop in quantity, drawing out a lot but infrequently might suit you.

How many bank accounts?

Before you retire, go through all your **financial resources** and see if they can be redistributed. It may be you have a number of building society accounts, all with smallish sums in them, which would be better put together as a larger sum that will attract higher interest overall. But if this means you spend all the interest instead of leaving some of it where it was, this may be a bad idea for you.

Perhaps you have two bank accounts and two cheque books? Would it be better to have just one and to take more care in your spending? Perhaps you have a large sum in a bank account that gains no interest but which would gain interest if it were in a different bank. You may be used to paying all bills by cheque and so have always kept a large sum in a current account. It might be better to put all this in a savings account and pay by cash. When you are retired you are more likely to have more time on your hands; going to a savings bank, drawing out the money and taking it direct to pay a bill will not only be cheaper but will give you a useful task to lend shape to your day.

There is no one answer as to how many bank or building society accounts you have; it all depends on how you feel about managing your money. One person may have all their money in a single building society; another may feel much better with it spread over six. The same is true of other places of deposit. But always remember that if someone else is looking after your money *they* should pay *you* for the privilege — and that goes for the commercial bank into which your wages have been paid all your life.

Investing for the future

Unless you continue to have a regular source of income well above your outgoings, investment will be an academic issue. Yet many people receive a **lump sum** on retirement which is worth investing because it is really part of the pension and intended to provide income. Do take advice as to how to invest it, from a reputable firm or individual consultant.

- If your **company offers help with financial advice** you would be wise to accept it; it will probably be the cheapest advice you can get and the best. In this case, invest as much as you can for both capital growth and income.
- Remember — *no financial advice is either free or disinterested.* Financial advisers always earn a percentage on the deals they complete, so at the very best you pay indirectly (for instance by paying a higher premium or getting less interest than you might do otherwise). But the fact that there is a cost — and it usually is quite a small and insignificant cost — should not deter you from taking advice.

Avoid like the plague any 'financial consultant' who is not recommended by someone you trust financially. If necessary take your bank manager's advice as to who might be a reliable financial consultant. But be careful about taking his own advice on how to invest — because every bank has its own schemes, and quite naturally it is in the interests of your bank manager to recommend them, but they might turn out to be quite costly.

Remember, too, that there is no certainty about investment of any kind. There is no such thing as a 'guaranteed return' on investment before you have invested. Projections of interest returns are no more than hopes, even if they are based on financial history. The life assurance company that is doing best this year may not be doing so well in six years' time.

Where to put your money

It is almost impossible to give advice as to where you should place your money for safe-keeping. However, you should always have some available for ready, even instant, access and the rest available with reasonable ease. What these sums should be will depend on your needs and lifestyle but most retired people should have at least £1,000 available on demand, apart from their normal banking/savings.

If you have been able to save by paying in to **life policies** of one sort or another it is good if they can mature sequentially — say one a year. And you may want to reinvest so that money becomes available in that way. There are various schemes including **National Savings Income Bonds,** but do examine your tax position as some schemes are more favourable than others, depending on your total income.

By and large you will want to put your money where it remains 'cash' rather than into goods or property. Even if property increases in value there are usually problems of selling and you may not be able to get your money quickly enough or with as high a return as you may need. Antiques and collectables are also subject to fickle markets and unless you have invested long before retirement it is unlikely you will come to understand the market quickly enough in retirement.

Of course, you may not wish to squeeze every last percentage out of your money. An odd half a per cent here and there may not be of much consequence and watching **interest fluctuations** may be an irritation. In this case you have simply to watch your spending. After all if you reach the end of each month without any debt you are doing fine, and that may be much healthier than anxiously adding up your interest at each month end.

There are various **options** for savings and investment but they do rather depend on how much money you have available over and above your regular running costs. Regular savings may be put into

- bank savings schemes (where interest is paid without deduction of tax)
- building society accounts which offer a wide variety of schemes and varied interest rates (and where interest is paid with tax deducted)
- insurance linked schemes (usually with a building society)
- Index Linked Save as You Earn
- Unit Trust regular savings schemes

Sums (such as lump sums on retirement) of under £1,000 are best invested in **National Savings Certificates, Bank Deposit Accounts,** or short loan (eg 7 day) **Building Society** accounts. The same sum may be invested for longer periods advantageously in **National Savings Certificates, National Savings Index Linked Certificates** (Granny Bonds), or **National Savings Deposit Bonds.**

Sums of over £1,000 may be best invested in **National Savings Income Bonds, Building Society Fixed Notice Shares,** or **Bank High Interest Cheque Accounts** (though these are only worth doing for substantial sums). Some other options which are high risk and which may appeal to those with a considerable surplus are shares, some unit trusts, investments trusts and the speculative areas such as antiques, paintings, jewellery and fine art in general; but one should have some knowledge of both the articles and the market to do this without great risk.

Creative accounting

Once you are retired and can organise your time more to your own convenience, you can save a lot of expense by **creative accounting.** This means you kill two financial birds with one stone and make one pound do the work of three. It sounds magical but it is not. It is based on the idea that a phone call at five *past* six is cheaper than one at five *to* six; that making *one bus trip* to town to pay the bills at each month end is cheaper than paying *each bill* as soon as it comes. Some people would call this simple thrift. How you do your creative accounting is up to you and is largely an attitude of mind; but a little thought will save pounds for the person who previously never gave true costs a thought.

Discounts for pensioners

Creative accounting would take into account the various concessions for pensioners such as

- reduced fares at certain times
- reduced entrance fees at unpopular hours
- special rates just because you are over 60 or 65

Some pensioners do not like it to be known that they are pensioners so they pay the full rate. Or they will not admit to themselves that their social status has changed so they pay over the odds. But everyone is entitled to age benefits at different times of their lives. Most students delight at *their* concessions so there is no need for older people to be too proud to accept them as well. After all, they are theirs by right.

Some **banks offer concessions** to customers over retirement age. For example, the Midland Bank offers an advisory service to anyone over the age of 55 and additional concessions to those over 60 (women) or 65 (men). Long-standing customers can probably do a deal with their local bank manager, especially with regard to interest charges which are usually negotiable anyway.

Travel **concessions** available to pensioners include

● bus passes in many local authority areas
● British Rail cards for cheap rail travel, though with some restrictions
● air travel (with British Airways there is a major reduction on any full normal round trip fare within the UK, though with certain time restrictions)
● continental travel discounts obtained through national travel bureaux
● reduced rates on Sealink ships to the Channel Islands, Isle of Man and Irish ports

Certain concessions are available in **medical matters.** All people of pensionable age (60 or 65 according to gender) are entitled to free medical prescriptions. In many areas chiropody services are free, as are dental and optical services. Full details can be obtained from your local Department of Health and Social Security (DHSS).

Shopping economically

Shopping economically is a gift that some people seem to have and others do not. One shopper can make a pound do what another makes fifty pence do; it is not a matter of gender at all, for women are no better at shopping than men or men than women. The way to check how good a shopper you are is to check up on your waste — how much (and of what) do you throw away in a week? And check on your clothes — how often do you wear a certain suit or coat?

● If you know you are a poor shopper go out with someone who is a good shopper and watch them in action. Do they choose cheaper brands, smaller quantities of perishable goods and larger quantities of durable goods? Do they only buy 'bargains' when they would have bought them anyway and ignore special offers? Watch carefully and learn.

There are many false economies but we all need to learn what they are. Some bulk purchases are good, others are bad. Some goods are sensibly bought and stored (such as wines and toilet rolls) while others are a waste (flour and paint). But a well-stocked larder is an investment; you can always make a meal at no apparent cost, while popping out to the local take-away or chip shop can cost several pounds.

Clothes, too, need care in purchasing. Both men and women are subject to fashion influences and too many clothes bought at one time mean too many clothes you won't want to wear later on. If you have the choice, have a small wardrobe and buy for each season; don't stock up with too many of this year's bargains because you will only want just as many of next year's. If you are not handy yourself with needle and cotton find a neighbour who is and pay them to do little alteration jobs for you. This way you will be able to buy good bargains and also have clothes that look good on you.

Checklist Financial Security
☐ Completed a 'personal financial audit'?
☐ Considered how to make the best use of financial resources in retirement?
☐ Worked out a rough annual budget?
☐ Money working efficiently — bank accounts, savings, investment?
☐ Some 'creative accounting' ideas to try?
☐ Taken advantage of professional advice?
☐ Financial security now under control?
☐ Checked the addresses/contacts at the back of this book?

Questionnaire

Accomplishment	Usefulness
good talker	teaching, lecturing
good writer	journalism, authorship
good with money	financial advice, investment, business
good with people	community work, business, teaching, counselling
well travelled	living overseas, working overseas
good qualifications, good work experience	business consultant, lecturing, teaching
good organiser	voluntary work, local affairs, business, clubs
good local knowledge	tourism, selling, social work
practical handyman	small business, odd-jobbing, voluntary help schemes
....	....
....	....
....	....
....	....
....	....
....	....
....	....
....	....
....	....
....	....
....	....
....	....
....	....
....	....
....	....
....	....
....	....
....	....
....	....
....	....

3
Personal Resources

Retirement is a key *stage* in life rather than a total change. It is important to remember this because many people view retirement as if they were about to be cut off from much of what went before and they forget that a great deal of previous experience is there to be drawn on. In fact, retirement is probably the first time in our life when we can draw on *all* our skills, talents and interests and organise them into a coherent and purposeful life scheme. In retirement we build on the firm foundations of our past, using our emotions, intellect and skills.

Try listing your major **accomplishments.** Note how you could use them in retirement. Some ideas are given on the opposite page to start you off.

Personal resources as wealth

People sometimes think of wealth as being a matter of money. Some retired people can become rather obsessed with money for a number of (often) good reasons. But wealth is not just money nor is it just good health, though it does encompass an adequacy of them. Many people suffer poor health, and everyone is ill from time to time, but that does not mean they lack wealth. Our real wealth is our resourcefulness and the emotional resilience that lets us draw on our **personal resources** which we tend to take for granted.

What are these personal resources? To begin with they are our natural instincts to survive, those energies that carry us through the day and which have served us so well over the years. The beauty of being a mature person is that so many of life's experiences have already come to us and we have passed through them stronger for the experience. Don't let's underestimate the value of a good deal of learning. Some of these experiences may have been traumatic in that they will have affected us very deeply — marriage, moving jobs, moving house, sickness, bereavement, children leaving home, divorce, financial problems. But however unpleasant and difficult they were at the time, we develop new inner strength as a result.

Try listing the six or seven most significant events in your life and then reflect what you have learned from each of them. To help you start, some examples are given.

Learning from life experience

The experience	The learning
Getting married	Working in partnership
Having children	Character building
Bereavement	Skills of understanding
	Coping with distress
	Developing self-reliance
Redundancy	Resolve
	Financial skills
	Resourcefulness
Moving away from home	Gaining independence
	Making friends
Divorce	Building a new life
	Developing new interests
Financial problems	Better financial skills, contacts and experience
Starting a business	Risk-taking and control
	Financial judgment

....
....
....
....
....
....
....
....
....
....
....
....
....
....
....
....

Emotional resources

We are all basically emotional and instinctive creatures. However rational we may be, unless there is a sound *emotional* basis for our decisions and attitudes they will be defective. We have to learn to deal with our emotional self before we can be rational or sensible. One advantage of maturity is that one has been able to recognise the emotional side of oneself and this recognition becomes a positive strength.

There are two practical aspects of understanding our emotions.

- One is in **understanding how we are affected by events** around us that give us pleasure or pain. Enjoying the sun shining on the garden, anticipating the pleasure of friends coming to visit, settling down to a good book or television programme — these are all emotional responses which help us to enjoy the world around us. Equally, emotional responses can be unpleasant, but they can still help us to evaluate what we do. Deciding to cut the grass before it starts to rain rather than leaving it too late when we will resent our own postponement may be an example.

- The second aspect relates to **decision-making.** Few decisions are made on the basis of pure fact or rationality. Most are made in terms of preferences and emotional dispositions. The example of cutting the grass is one way this happens. Most positive decisions are made on the basis of preference; it is a nice day so let's go out for a drive; or it is a wet day so we decide not even to post a letter.

But emotions also affect negative decisions and these can be harder to deal with. On a cold, damp day we may decide not to go to the art exhibition we have been looking forward to. So we stay in and mope. When our time is our own we are more prone to let negative feelings control us than positive ones. Yet our whole life experience should have taught us that it is always better to do something rather than do nothing. Most of the time we can manage our feelings very well, but we need to be vigilant that we do not get into careless ways.

Another effect of understanding one's own emotions is that we can start to understand other people. If we don't understand our own feelings they get mixed up with other people's and we cannot be objective. We become easily led into bad emotional responses. Maturity should bring with it tolerance and understanding of others and this can only happen when we understand our own feelings and lose any need to project them onto other people.

For instance, it can be very tempting to become impatient with assistants in shops, banks, cafes and so on, particularly if they are slow or careless. It is natural to get annoyed but since annoyance achieves nothing it is better to be understanding. From our own long experience we know that myriad things can go wrong in a day and what private things can affect our mood at work. How often have *we* been curt or impatient with customers and clients? We can be understanding of others when the roles are reversed.

Of all the emotions a good sense of humour is the most precious. To have a sense of humour one needs to be relaxed and at ease with oneself. (Telling jokes is perhaps different; that might require tenseness or anger since much humour is critical or angry.) A sense of humour is a sense of enjoyment of life itself; it is the ability to turn potentially hurtful events into harmless ones. If you slip on the pavement you laugh and don't become angry at the idiot who dropped the orange peel. If you miss the bus you find something enjoyable to do until the next one. If you get drenched in the rain you can still laugh because you look such a fright.

It is unlikely that in retirement the detail of anything you do will be much different from what you have experienced some time in your life and so you should know what to do as soon as you recognise it.

● Imagine the worst thing that could possibly happen to you. In what ways could it be 'tragic' and in what ways 'comic'? Try to be objective!

Intellectual resources

Sometimes people fear that their **intellectual powers** will diminish with age. This is not so except in the sense that brain cells have been dying since our late teens! *Memory* may change a little so that you temporarily forget things that happened recently but this won't materially affect your intellectual performance. Young people can have much worse memory problems than quite elderly people and most 'intellectual' problems have an emotional basis.

Intellectual powers should always be perfectly adequate for what you want to do, though it's worth remembering that some things you used to do will no longer be of much significance to you. But if you continue with intellectual interests that were strong before retirement there will be no significant impairment. If you have had a lifelong interest in antiques you will be able to remember all you need.

The most important quality of mind is intellectual *curiosity*. This means taking an interest in everything going on around you, particularly in what people you know are doing. It is well worth reading a daily newspaper (however much it may at times irritate you) and watching the TV news. Local newspapers are also a source of stimulus because they let you know what is going on nearer home. Free newspapers, which are now almost universal, are a good source of trivial but interesting local information.

Local radio, of course, can be a most informative companion.

Intellectual curiosity has enormous value. Even a walk into town can be full of interest; if you do not meet anyone there are still gardens to look at, houses to observe with their architectural features, traffic and tradesmen. Indeed, many elderly people love to live on a main road, simply because so much of interest goes by. Our intellectual curiosity links us with the world and presents us with opportunities.

Using our intellect can lead us into new worlds of absorbing involvement, too. We can take up new interests which may call for considerable skill. Business opportunities we will look at in Chapter 8 but here our theme is general intellectual awareness, which for many retired people can be as lively as when they first went to school.

Some people take up a musical instrument; others take up all kinds of other demanding projects. There is no slackening of standards; beginners are beginners however old they are, and after that every stage of accomplishment is possible. Not everyone who plays the piano will reach concert standard but that doesn't mean they can't play pretty well after a year or two.

Perhaps most important of all is that retired people should join **groups of people of all ages.** While inevitably some things will be done in groups with other retired people, where possible try and mix with younger *and* older people. Except for the old and sick, retirement clubs have very little real use. The best way of thinking about retirement is not to think of it as 'retirement' but rather as the next natural stage in life.

Skill resources

All retired people have a range of technical skills of all sorts that they have learned over many years. Some may be lying dormant, having been unused for a long time; others will be of recent use and well developed. Most people — but by no means everyone — discover they have quite a lot of **practical ability** and in retirement there is usually more opportunity to use it. However, it is more than likely the skills are gender-orientated; that is, there are some skills which are thought to be men's skills and some women's. Cooking (women) and carpentry (men) are two obvious examples. In retirement the gender orientation often breaks down and men begin to do 'women's jobs' while women do men's — though sometimes this is out of necessity rather than preference.

Certainly retirement is a good time to think about re-allocating domestic jobs. The best solution is for everyone to take turns with every job but certainly no job should be left only to one sex. Men can become just as good at making beds and ironing as women and women can change electric plugs and put up kitchen shelves with as much ease as a man. As for painting the house, it is simply a matter of who has the better head for heights.

*"He won't even let me get in
the kitchen now!"*

There are three categories of skill for those in retirement.

- Firstly, **skills we have already learned** and continue with because they are immediately useful. For many people gardening skills will be of this nature; so will letter writing.
- Secondly, **skills we have started to learn** and which can be developed. Domestic skills will usually fall in this category; extending one's capability at cooking would be an example.
- Thirdly, there are **new skills** that may have to be learned from scratch; computer and word processor skills might fall into this category.

The important thing is to make sure that one is functioning in all three categories most of the time — something continued, something improved and something learned.

Alongside these technical skills we need to extend and refine our **social skills.** The basis of this is to avoid any sense of being a special category of person — 'retired'. Nothing is more irritating than for people to insist on their status — whatever that may be. We do not expect the people we meet in the ordinary ways of things to say 'I'm chairman of a large and prestigious company', or, 'Of course, I'm 35 you know.' So we should not gratuitiously offer the information, 'Of course, I'm retired now'; it implies that you expect some special consideration for that reason alone. The important thing about social skills for retired people is that they should see themselves in the same ways as anyone else — just enjoying the life they have been given.

Time for a change
We are never too old to change. Some people think that at a certain point in one's life one reaches 'maturity' and stays there for the rest of one's life. Some people do this in their early twenties and just stop developing.

One of the wonderful things about being human is our endless ability to **change and adapt;** that means we have an infinite capacity to learn. Some people even seem to wait until retirement in order to start being what they have always wanted to be and often cause considerable surprise to their friends. As we get older, it becomes increasingly important for us to maintain our emotional resilience and capacity to change because there is no less need to change in relation to the world around us.

Let's use our capacity to change positively when deciding what we do and where we go. There is never any need to feel ashamed or even childish in wanting to move on to new experiences. The chances are that we will do much more than just 'cope', and most of us will find ourselves very much at home in our new milieu.

Rich home environment

As we go through life we accumulate lots of possessions (and junk). In retirement we may be less acquisitive but we will still acquire things. One thing we will acquire is more time to ourselves. Many retired people claim that they never have any spare time; that they don't know how they ever found time for work before retirement. But they can say this because they are busy, which is a state they have created for themselves. They surround themselves with stimulating people and activities.

However busy one is, there will always be time when one is left to one's own resources. It is then that the quality of one's material accumulations become important. This is when the stamp collection comes into its own, the antique books can be carefully examined, the record collection drawn on, books taken off the shelves for a first reading. The quality of domestic environment is even more important in retirement than during earlier working life. But domestic environment doesn't just happen; it cannot be created in a moment. Making sure that one's future needs will be well provided for is an essential pre-retirement task, because one's intellectual and cultural life is all of a piece.

Sex differentiation

We have already mentioned sex differences in relation to tasks about the house. One of the problems of retirement is that our *culture* does not give equality of opportunity or provision to men and women. Since women live longer than men, and so there are many more of them in old age, women may receive more care and attention. But there is a danger that many women shelter within the female stereotype and accentuate their subordinate role in retirement. Many men take advantage of this, making only token gestures towards sexual equality, for instance, by sharing in domestic chores without really sharing responsibilities.

Retirement for both men and women should be a period of **developing**

independence and the creating of new roles and interests. Men may as likely have to be nursemaids to sick wives as the other way round. Some, rather than daughters, may have to nurse sick mothers. But there may be other fruitful forms of role reversal such as the wife taking on a full-time job as her retirement business while the husband takes on a domestic role.

● In retirement many of the entrenched social problems and attitudes can be faced with a **new spirit** and many important social and cultural leads given that younger people are too timid to attempt.

In many ways, retirement offers a period of considerable **security and stability.** We are inclined to think of it as a period when we are more vulnerable to economic and social pressures. But this is not so; many people in competitive mid-career have greater anxieties and with good reason. In retirement most of us know where we are and have a good idea of where we are going to be in the months, even years, ahead. Many young people have less certainty.

Retirement should be a time for careful and calculated experiment — and sometimes thoughtless abandon! Retired people can offer many wise and experienced comments on society at large, and have a chance to put into practice some of the most cherished ideals and hopes of earlier life. Younger people should be able to observe — even envy — real fulfilment in their elders and they should be seeing that the later years of life are as full of adventure and success as any other time.

Checklist
Using your personal resources

☐ Thought about accomplishments and how to use them?
☐ Considered how a lifetime's experiences can be drawn upon?
☐ Balanced emotional outlook and understanding of other people?
☐ Intellectual interests to continue?
☐ Active (and dormant) skills to apply?
☐ Ready to adapt and change?
☐ Quality of home and domestic life?
☐ Checked the addresses/contacts at the back of this book?

4
Travel and Holidays

Perhaps one of the features most looked forward to in retirement is the opportunity — the many opportunities — to travel and take more holidays and breaks than during working life. Previously time off work had to be arranged to fit in with awkward constraints such as the office holiday rota or holiday weeks in the town. For many people there was a dead period over the Christmas and New Year holiday period, while summer holidays were dominated by family requirements.

Only occasionally could one take a break out of season, getting the best bargains — though not necessarily the best weather. But for many people when the time comes to take holidays just when they wish the will is often lacking to do something different and exciting; this can be largely related to lack of experience in holiday planning during earlier life.

Holiday interests

For some people, choosing a place to retire to is one way of creating opportunities for holidaying. One couple took the chance in mid-career to move into a small business in the English Lake District, because they so much enjoyed fell-walking and hill-climbing that they decided to blend work and play during their working life.

● There is everything to be said for making such physical changes well *before* actual retirement though one is, as a consequence, limited to holidaying in the chosen area probably for the rest of one's life!

It's well worth considering one's **outdoor lifestyle** in good time and making appropriate arrangements. Someone who loves speaking a European language might consider moving to one of the towns on the south coast from which ferry trips are easily possible; some day trips are virtually free by the time duty-free concessions have been taken into account.

Those who have outdoor interests of a specific kind may well have already let their interests determine their career and where they live.

Farmers, horticulturalists, foresters, and nature wardens are some of those for whom the links between work and personal interest are close. Others may have an affinity for another country and may start their move in mid career. Perhaps their interest in Etruscan remains is such that they buy a small house or farm in Tuscany. Or they love swimming and sailing so they buy a villa on a Greek island.

But such people are not just buying a holiday cottage in an attractive part of Europe; they have a genuine functional interest that can only be satisfied by living abroad and by becoming an active part of the community.

"We just can't stand the pace!"

Living abroad

Many people make the mistake of buying an apartment abroad (Malta, Portugal, Spain are the commonest places) where there is an **English community.** They often reckon that the purchase is a bargain by UK standards and like the idea of lying in the sun all day long and joining in an endless round of cocktail and dinner parties. Such decisions tend to be regretted because these **expatriates** never become a part of local life; tax advantages may change and the popularity of the 'incomers' with the locals may decline. Furthermore, when one spouse dies the other can be exceedingly lonely.

People who simply buy a holiday cottage abroad may never really become part of the community; they may be considered undesirable 'absentee residents' by the locals and discover that they do not want to live there after all.

In any case the renewal of the expatriate community can only be effected by more retired people and if the popularity of the place falls off, the Brits become a rapidly dwindling part of the community. On the other hand if arrangements can be made for a temporary residence overseas, with a return to Britain after a year or two guaranteed, the arrangement might work. And those three-month holidays out of season on the Spanish coast for older Britons are a good bargain and worth anyone's try, at least once in a while.

Cruises

Some people choose to go on cruises as a way of celebrating their retirement. They may fulfil a life-time ambition and take a world cruise or a Mediterranean cruise on some great cruise ship. Certainly if you have plenty of money this can be a good idea though it may not turn out quite as expected.

For one thing, cruise passengers tend to be elderly and there is always a proportion of the international idle rich with whom it may be difficult to make satisfactory social contact. (The problem is not their being rich but their being 'idle'!) A cruise is not the best way of seeing the world, though certainly it may be the most comfortable way. But it is also very expensive and can be quite a drain on retirement capital. For instance £1,000 spent on a cruise is worth about £2,000 over eight or nine years if invested and/or differently spent. It is all a matter of creative accounting as discussed in Chapter 2.

Extended leisure

The danger of letting retirement disintegrate into continuous leisure is a grave one. Physical and emotional decline develops imperceptibly among those whose only object in life is to play. Pure play lacks stimulation and the basic dynamic for personal development. There's far more to living than just being a 'playboy'.

Of course, extended leisure is one of the great benefits of retirement but overextended leisure will not bring desired happiness. On the other hand, a long period of recuperation after an illness can be one of the rewards of retirement; in retirement one can taste the fruits of leisure to the full.

Travel discounts

Not everyone who has retired will be in receipt of a state pension, because they may be below the statutory retirement age. This means they will not be eligible for special reductions on travel (unless they are under 25!)

However, older people between the magic discount ages may well find they qualify for other forms of discount. Anyone travelling extensively within the United States may find they qualify for free air travel and there are always travel bargains for foreign nationals in all countries, especially on railways, but sometimes on planes. There are many kinds of travel discount and special bargains though they do take a bit of researching. Travel bargains are a maze even for experts. Since part of the fun of travel is making the arrangements, there can be a great deal of pleasure and satisfaction in finding special facilities and opportunities.

Using travel agents

Travel agents themselves do not know all the answers to travel opportunities, and your local travel agent will have links with certain providers and not others. If you really are interested in travel, why not set about becoming your own expert? It is not too difficult and if you are a railway buff and enjoy reading railway timetables there are enormous pleasures to be found.

There is no reason for a retired person to go straight into the local travel agent, asking for what they have. Try to go in much more *prepared,* know what you want and ask the clerk to book it for you. Agents get their commission on everything they sell so it is no loss to them if you tell them which route you want to go and at what times. Even on the various Channel crossings there are often bargains hidden away in the brochures that the hard-pressed package-tour seller does not know about.

But it's worth using agents as much as possible because they are an additional source of information. If you get to know your local agents they will be able to help you even more and will welcome the challenge of dealing with someone well informed. They may even be able to advise you of bargains you would otherwise have missed. And if you are really keen on travel you might like to try organising trips for parties of friends; if the party is over a certain size (usually somewhere between 10 and 30) there will be a free place for you. It sounds easy to arrange tours and holidays; but you will certainly earn your money. You have only to be let down by one person and your whole profit has gone.

Home travel

Overseas travel sounds exciting and sometimes exotic but it can only be a small part of the travel that most of us do. If we travel too much we neglect our home and local life which we need for continual emotional support. Home travel includes that in the locality which is functional or for leisure, as well as travel for holidays or to visit family or friends. It is nice if we can achieve a good balance of all kinds. Some people make a point of regular local travel, visiting a different place every week for shopping or just a day out. If we look back over a year and look at our travel pattern we can see if we could make some creative economies or add some additional purpose.

- How well do you know your **local area**?
- Try keeping a travel diary and use a travel planner. See how much **creative travelling** is open to you each year.
- How about starting a file at home to keep all the **travel brochures and information** you can collect?

Some people take retirement as an opportunity to visit places they have never been to before and aim gradually to cover the British Isles on visits and holidays of one sort or another. If you are interested in country houses you might want to plan trips around them. If interested in fishing you might want to try new rivers or canals. If you play golf you might want to play on all the municipal golf courses or all the Scottish courses. If you are a bird watcher you might want to visit each major sanctuary once a year. If your interest is in gardening then you might want to organise your holidays around the great plant and tree collections of the country.

Of local interest in many towns are **Town Trails** which enable you to visit all the most notable buildings in a systematic way. If your town does not have one you could write one yourself, or write an additional specialised one (eg noting shop frontages, pointing out street furniture). All towns offer more to the visitor than shops, and an interest in urban architecture adds a new dimension to enjoying any town in any country. Why not seek the help of your local library or museum?

Shopping

Shopping can be organised around the various **market days and fairs** in the locality. You might use the **county shows** to replenish the garden. Then there are the **specialist fairs** like Preston Pot Fair where you can find useful things at bargain prices. Other people explore the supermarkets in turn; many of them provide free bus travel from one part of the town to another. Or you might want to visit the English Hypermarkets scattered throughout the country. They are different from the French ones but often situated in out-of-town shopping centres. Given the vagaries of the English climate, these large shopping centres such as Brent Cross, Gateshead Metro Centre and Telford Town Centre provide ideal rendezvous for weekly shopping and there is no problem about making them 'a day out'. A number of factory shops serve the same purpose and are often visited by coachloads of day trippers (such as the famous 'Tommy Balls' at Blackburn).

A sense of purpose

The secret of enjoying home travel is to make it purposeful. It makes routine shopping more interesting — though sometimes the local shopping centre is a welcome relief from travelling and finding car parks or waiting at bus and train stations — and it can fulfil some clear purpose related to a hobby. It could be rather dull visiting, for example, the newly created Heritage Centre (Wigan Pier, Styal Village, Liverpool's Albert Dock or London's St Catherine's Dock) only to look in the souvenir shops. But if one is a photographer and is creating a photographic essay, or a painter with an interest in certain subjects, then a visit tó such places is enriched tenfold.

If you enjoy visiting old places, consider doing this in association with a local historical society or WEA class. Often such groups will be doing actual research and may be preparing to publish booklets on a specialist topic.

A day out which would have been relaxing during a working year soon becomes tedious when it is one of a relentless stream of day visits undertaken just to fill the time. A sense of purpose makes all the difference.

Travel for travel's sake

Some people love to travel for its own sake and welcome retirement as a time when their interest can be extended. Some single people travel somewhere new every holiday throughout their working life and continue to do so in retirement. Some teachers and lecturers make certain that they visit a new country virtually every holiday and take three major holidays a year. Others visit another continent every other year on a special interest trip — sports, archaeology, gastronomy, photography, painting.

If your interest is **railways,** for example, the possibilities are endless.

There are a number of steam engine lines in both England and Wales. Some of the Little Railways of Wales are quite spectacular (a special brochure is available from the Welsh Tourist Board). You might also try to include some of the famous rail journeys of the world in your plans. The most famous, perhaps, of world rail journeys are the coast-to-coast route across Canada, the journey across the Nullabor Desert in Australia, the Blue Train in South Africa, the Lima (Peru) to La Paz (Bolivia), the tiny Palma to Soller line in Majorca and the now totally sanitised Orient Express, to mention just a few that will spring readily to mind. For one fascinating account, read Paul Theroux's *The Great Railway Bazaar.*

If **photography** is also a hobby, very interesting portfolios can be made up and, if transparencies are taken lectures can be given on the return home after one or more of these exotic journeys. (There is an unsatisfied demand for good lecturers for different kinds of organisations. But lecturers *must* be good at public speaking!) Those who enjoy **sketching** and prefer to travel at greater leisure might well consider travel to be a fruitful and rewarding basis for their hobby.

Bus travel is another possibility and might well include travel across the United States and Canada by Greyound and Grey Travel. Bus travel is also possible within Europe (to Paris and Amsterdam, for instance) and some may wish to travel to the Near or Far East by bus when the special services are running.

For the more wealthy and those who prefer to save up for their adventures to be taken in a different form of comfort, **air travel** can be used in a similar way. Even **river ferries** offer possibilities for there are quite a lot of interesting ferry services round the British coast. This could be enlivened by travel on some coastal **cargo boats** which still ply from port to port. Some cargo vessels to South America still take passengers and look after them very well. The Norwegian coast could be travelled using local shipping rather than by going on a 'midnight sun' package tour. Whatever mode of travel one chooses there is unlimited scope for the imagination.

Even **package tours** can be used creatively. One could cover the Spanish coast with little difficulty by using the cheapest package tours over a year or two. The French Atlantic Coast can be visited out of season on mini-trips — weekend and mid-week. Sometimes package tour operators offer an extra week free if you travel at an odd time of the year. And you can have several months in Canada quite cheaply if you go and return at the end of the season, or just spend a few days at an unpopular time of the year between main flight periods. Some cruises have standby fares that are quite cheap, even if you have to travel to another country to get them! And, of course, there are the flight-only bargains that drop you in the middle of Crete or Portugal and so force you to look for local accommodation.

Summer schools

A very good form of cheap travel is to attend summer schools of one sort or another. Often schools and conferences offer specially reduced rates for travel and hotels. One of you could attend a conference while your partner goes sight-seeing. International conferences often offer special rates to spouses, too, and organise — chauvinistically — special events for wives (and companions). Quite a number of international organisations hold worthwhile events and it is often possible to extend the visit considerably at either end of the event in order to do some local visiting and still benefit from the special fares.

In the United Kingdom the popularity of summer schools is increasing. Many universities offer programmes and a number of boarding (eg Millfield) and residential schools do likewise. One of the advantages is that you will meet a cross-the-ages group of people since many families go because there is something for everyone and the children can go off on their own.

Special interest weekends

Some hotel chains run special interest weekends which, while not particularly cheap, do offer something of interest in very comfortable surroundings. After all there is often not very much to do on a British country holiday particularly when it is raining; having events planned by the hotel can be welcome, and provide a chance to get to know other like-minded people.

Exchanges with friends

Where members of the family are living abroad, retired people often like to pay an extended visit. Some join **reunion clubs** to do this, but others just go on a cheaper or charter flight. Such a visit can be a highlight of the early years of retirement. One can also arrange a series of exchange visits with friends (or pen pals if this has been an interest). Exchanges have lots of positive points in their favour; they are reciprocal and you can offer in return an equivalent to what you receive but with the cost under your control. Many people would rather stay *en famille* than have to go sight-seeing all the time, and living with friends can be more fun than staying in hotels. How about taking in overseas guests for a summer or two, to see if any friendships develop that can lead to return visits, both ways?

Checklist
Travel and holidays

- ☐ Considered whether to move or to stay put?
- ☐ Living abroad — checked the possible pitfalls?
- ☐ Avoiding the trap of over-extended leisure?
- ☐ Checked travel discount facilities?
- ☐ Found a really good travel agent for advice?
- ☐ Discovered your own local area?
- ☐ Shopping — developed a new sense of purpose?
- ☐ Pros and cons of package tours and independent travel?
- ☐ Investigated opportunities at summer schools?
- ☐ Investigated possible exchanges with friends?
- ☐ Checked the addresses/contacts at the back of this book?

5
Opportunities at Home

One of the most welcome advantages of retirement is being able to spend more time at home. Home becomes the base from which all your new activities will be planned; it will be both home and office. There may be a temptation to treat being at home like one long Christmas holiday but it will soon become boring if you do. It might in fact be best to start your retirement with a holiday away, at least within a few weeks of retirement, and then start back as you mean to go on with a more systematically organised life.

There may be lots of little jobs to be done about the house, postponed over the last few years, and you may now want to get them done — rather in the way you might use a bank holiday to do things at home instead of getting caught up in traffic jams. But it would be a big mistake to organise your retirement around *only* doing jobs about the house. It is much better to treat the home as you have always done and, if you are a procrastinator, continue more or less like that.

The important thing about home is to make it only one of several locations for your activities. You still need to associate with other places for other interests. If you spend the whole day working at home it can be hard to relax in. There is nothing better in the late afternoon than having somewhere to go back to! For many people, actually setting out to work and getting ready to come back home are important daily routines.

JOBS ABOUT THE HOUSE

It is unlikely that you will discover a newfound enthusiasm for the home and the many jobs to be done if you have not already been used to doing them. If you have not systematically decorated the house room by room during your working life it is unlikely you will want to do so now, though for some people this sort of change will be suitable. Obviously, you have time now to do more little jobs but the bigger ones will still have to be done by someone else; you will need to budget for such jobs as outside painting, window replacements, the repair of the garage roof and so on.

But there are jobs that you may well take to. A little more painting of woodwork, cleaning ornaments and cupboards, sorting out the garage or garden shed. It is a good idea to make a list of all these 'annual' jobs and try to work through them systematically during the year. Since you are at home more often than before, many outside jobs that depend on good weather can now be done at the right time.

For other odd jobs it is a good idea to find someone local who will do them at a reasonable price whenever you want them. You may, of course, already have someone to do this but, if not, make it a priority to find a friendly local odd-job man, student or neighbour who will help out willingly.

Write down the jobs you *won't* do yourself. By each one note who you will ask to do it — and what it will cost! Keep a list of names and phone numbers handy beside the telephone. The list is started off for you.

Home improvements

Painting　　　　　　　　　　　＿＿＿＿＿＿＿＿＿＿＿
Decorating (paper hanging)　　＿＿＿＿＿＿＿＿＿＿＿
Electrical jobs　　　　　　　　＿＿＿＿＿＿＿＿＿＿＿
Central heating repairs　　　　＿＿＿＿＿＿＿＿＿＿＿
Joinery (shelves etc)　　　　　＿＿＿＿＿＿＿＿＿＿＿
Plumbing (frozen pipes)　　　　＿＿＿＿＿＿＿＿＿＿＿
Window repairs (broken panes)　＿＿＿＿＿＿＿＿＿＿＿

Other

. . . .　＿＿＿＿＿＿＿＿＿＿＿
. . . .　＿＿＿＿＿＿＿＿＿＿＿
. . . .　＿＿＿＿＿＿＿＿＿＿＿
. . . .　＿＿＿＿＿＿＿＿＿＿＿
. . . .　＿＿＿＿＿＿＿＿＿＿＿
. . . .　＿＿＿＿＿＿＿＿＿＿＿
. . . .　＿＿＿＿＿＿＿＿＿＿＿
. . . .　＿＿＿＿＿＿＿＿＿＿＿
. . . .　＿＿＿＿＿＿＿＿＿＿＿
. . . .　＿＿＿＿＿＿＿＿＿＿＿
. . . .　＿＿＿＿＿＿＿＿＿＿＿
. . . .　＿＿＿＿＿＿＿＿＿＿＿
. . . .　＿＿＿＿＿＿＿＿＿＿＿
. . . .　＿＿＿＿＿＿＿＿＿＿＿

Decorating

It is a good idea to have the house completely redecorated some time *before* the time of retirement. There are two reasons for this.

- One is to ensure that everything is clean, ship-shape and in order so that there are *no sudden unexpected expenses*. Some items may need attention because they are worn and becoming dangerous, such as stair carpets. There may be doors that need rehanging or steps that are becoming hazardous.

- The other reason is to **simplify the various finishes and surfaces** so that they can easily be repaired or painted without the whole room or house being done. Of course, questions of personal taste apply here but decorations and furnishings which are too fussy may cause expensive problems at a time when you don't feel like having to deal with them. It is also a good idea to check on the condition of upholstery that is going to be used a lot. You don't want your favourite chair to collapse and have to be replaced by one similar at ten times the original cost!

A good way of keeping the home looking fresh and comfortable is to aim at decorating (painting is easiest) one or two rooms a year with the downstairs or living rooms having priority. If the house is very big and the rooms large and airy you might do a wall every three months. The problem is that as you get older, and especially if you have a busy social life, the upset of decorating can be something you just don't want to face. In any case, when you do decorate it is a good idea to get someone to help you; perhaps a youngster from nearby or a grandson. And give them a few pounds for their pains. You will also get the job finished more quickly.

If you have been using a regular decorator for several years you can expect some advice and additional help, particularly if you have been able to recommend his services in the past to other neighbours. Sometimes painters and odd-job men will quote a better price if several of you have a job done at the same time. But be as cautious as ever of men who come to the door with an immediate and pressing offer. Rogues are no respecters of age.

If you have not bothered with **wall insulation** or **double-glazing,** you are unlikely to benefit from them now. It will be a waste of money, so save that lump sum when the offers come through the door or the salesman calls. It takes about ten years to get the monetary value back at the best of times. In any case older people who have not had these improvements tend not to notice any disadvantage. However, if you do not have **central heating** it could be worthwhile having it installed; but have thermal controls on each radiator, to help control the cost.

It is also worth considering the general convenience of the home should someone become ill or an invalid. In this respect the **bathroom** is particularly important; make sure the bath is one that an elderly person can use with safety. Perhaps it would be worth having a new bath fitted, with grab handles.

The kitchen
Once you are retired, the kitchen will become more important. How about developing a real interest in good cooking and food preparation? In most households one person tends to be 'proprietor' — and for very good working reasons — but the kitchen should now be used by everyone according to their interests. It may be worth making some improvements to the kitchen though there is no need to have it fully refitted. But it can be made more labour saving and convenient. Investment in a microwave oven may be worthwhile, particularly if you live alone or one of you lunches alone. Check that all your equipment is in good order and if necessary buy a new set of non-stick pans — or ask for them as a leaving present. Make sure you have good knives; blunt ones are more dangerous than sharp ones.

The kitchen is the most creative room in the house and used at all times of the day, in all seasons and on all occasions. If you can eat in the kitchen, as well as cook, you are well set up for a busy social life!

There is nowhere in the home more *versatile* than the kitchen though there are some things better done in the garage or shed. (Where do you clean your shoes or repair the vacuum cleaner?) There will always be things to buy — gadgets or equipment (friends and family should never have difficulty over presents for you). You will be able to derive enormous pleasure from doing things in the kitchen; one can never know too much about cooking.

Making furnishings
Not everyone is handy with a needle but that is no reason why things should not be *made for the house*. Many men discover that they have skills with needles and scissors that they never realised. Often the awareness comes when a wife's failing eyesight means she has to ask her husband to sew his shirt buttons on. From there he can progress to more ambitious tasks. Making curtains is one way to start learning, shortening trousers is another. Many men actually start with some quite dramatic project like upholstery because they can join an evening class and actually complete covers for a settee and chairs by the end of the year.

Other things which could be done are making cushions (tapestry or fabric), making rugs, making a bed cover. And there is no reason why knitting should be left to the women in the house; men are perfectly capable of knitting pullovers — or at the very least a scarf. These activities, and similar ones like embroidery and crochet, have the added advantage that they keep the fingers and wrists supple and can, for example, be done in bed if one is recovering from 'flu.

KEEPING THE HOME ALIVE

There is some danger of letting domestic activities fall into abeyance after retirement. The home can become more of a museum than a hive of activity. Some people may stop taking an interest in their way of life and stop buying anything new. It is still important to **replace things** that are old, to **improve the facilities** where possible, and to **show freshness and interest.** Fresh flowers about the house are in important sign of domestic vitality. There will always be some branches, twigs and flowers somewhere in the garden or the hedgerow; wild flowers can be changed every other day and will always give pleasure.

Plants, too, bring life to the house. Though most house plants tend to be foliage plants, there are inexpensive plants that flower and something can be found for all seasons. Good flowering plants include begonias, cyclamens, streptocarpus and primula. Fresh flowers add life to a home and in the winter months bulbs can be substituted and used outside eventually.

Pictures, too, play an important part in creating atmosphere. Oddly, perhaps, few people change them once they have been hung. In some towns it is possible to rent or borrow pictures. Pictures make good conversation pieces so it is nice to have a change from time to time. Calendars are good for conversation too and can often be linked with other interests — places where you have holidayed or where family members or friends live.

Books and magazines

The British are not renowned for their book buying but there are plenty of well-stocked **public libraries.** Aside from having a book 'on the go' a visit to the library can become a social event. Books help to awaken and maintain interests and provide something new to talk about. Buying books is also fun and a browse in a new or secondhand **bookshop** can make many a town visit worthwhile; it is certainly a good way to stay out of the rain. If you buy paperback novels you might join a syndicate of people who pass them round; this can create an occasion for a visit, a chat and a drink. If you like hardbacks it might be worth joining a **book club** because hardback books come at bargain prices — and you can buy some of your Christmas presents that way.

Most people take a daily (morning or evening) newspaper, often for something quite specific like the sport or crossword. A newspaper through the door in the morning, like the postal delivery, is a contact with the world outside. Newspapers are probably the best way of being kept informed about the world in general but it can be a good idea in retirement to take one or more magazines because this too will keep you informed and stimulated. Again, you might form a syndicate for sharing one or more magazines. The *Which* series is one of the best for a group of friends or neighbours.

A few books and magazines scattered about the house are useful to help visitors feel at home, especially if they have to be left alone. And they provide talking points for conversation.

Music

Some people build a record collection with retirement in mind. One could easily collect thousands of records in a lifetime, but which would take another lifetime to listen to! Now that compact discs have arrived, the quality of recording does not deteriorate and there is an abundance of music of all kinds. Even if you have few records yourself, you can borrow them from your local record library or join a commercial record library which will also offer discounts on purchases.

Listening to music is one of the delights of life whether you are retired or not, and it is certainly worth cultivating in retirement. Even if the living room is small, one can listen to music by using earphones while others watch television. Investing in new hi-fi equipment may be worthwhile for many people; and extension loudspeakers in the kitchen can be fitted. The older one gets the more one appreciates good quality music and the radio.

Music is nowadays an acceptable background to conversation, often making it easier for people to get into conversation. It also forms a talking point. Exchanging records and tapes (the indestructible compact discs come into their own here) can be an important part of social relationships. Why not invite friends and neighbours in to listen to new discs? The quality of background music in the house can be a significant contributor to the quality of life.

Entertaining

One is never too old to entertain. In the early days of retirement some people feel like putting on spectacular dinner parties or buffets; but as one gets older the desire for upsets in the kitchen will diminish. But there are lots of ways of entertaining that are neither costly nor troublesome. Each of us can develop our own ideas of entertainment and we should not undervalue the importance of impromptu entertaining.

Some people like to protect their privacy and welcome visitors only by invitation; others keep open house. Others adopt a systematic approach to inviting different groups of friends; some use the occasion of staying

How will I entertain?

Try matching friends against the following:

Hospitality	To be invited
morning coffee	_____
lunch	_____
afternoon tea	_____
high tea	_____
evening meal or dinner	_____
supper	_____
picnic	_____
garden drinks	_____
Sunday morning drinks	_____
dinner party	_____
party	_____

guests to entertain their local friends. And, of course, in the summer every kind of outdoor entertainment is possible from coffee or iced drinks, through barbecues to formal garden parties. But everyone can call on a neighbour to share a cup of tea. In retirement the impromptu social gathering often becomes more possible.

Home interests

We become so used to our home and our way of life that we seldom think it can have any interest to anyone else. Yet all of us have a natural curiosity about other people's homes and most of us enjoy a visit just to have a look. In our domestic lives we express ourselves more fully than perhaps we realise and an invitation into the home is a very complete way of sharing ourselves with others. *Every* home has something of interest and charm to offer the visitor; let's take delight in sharing what we have. Books and records have already been mentioned. Collections — paintings, ornaments, keepsakes — are others, and visitors may be delighted to enjoy our 'collections' with us.

It is worth reviewing our possessions simply to make ourself aware again of the wonderful things that surround us and to take note of the resources that we so often take for granted. Here is a random list of some of the things there may be in a home that would give delight to someone else, perhaps a neighbour, perhaps a child — binoculars, telescope, old camera, musical box, mechanical toys, model railway, model ship, souvenirs from overseas. What can be found in *your* home? — you might be surprised!

Sharing one's home

Few people in retirement want to take in permanent lodgers or rent out rooms unless there is financial need. Indeed, where there is a financial transaction involving property the advice of a solicitor should definitely be asked. But there are ways of sharing a home, if only for brief periods. The meeting of new people that this involves can be enormously rewarding even if it restricts one's own movements.

How about taking in a college or university student for one or more terms? Terms only last from ten to twelve weeks and leave the long holiday periods free. A young person may be a welcome temporary addition to the home; a relative or friend may fit the bill. Or you may like to take a young worker who has come to town either on a course or who is looking for somewhere permanent to live. You might consider overseas visitors who are on vacation or you may take overseas students on a short language course. Taking in a paying guest just once in a lifetime is a contribution to society that can also give personal satisfaction. Retired people who live alone could find taking a guest as rewarding as a married couple would.

Checklist
Opportunities at Home

- ☐ Ready to use home as a base?
- ☐ List of jobs to do about the house?
- ☐ Someone to help with odd jobs?
- ☐ House redecorated before retirement?
- ☐ The right fixtures and fittings for a comfortable retirement?
- ☐ Kitchen and entertainment area in good order?
- ☐ Practice with new home and DIY skills?
- ☐ Reading materials, music/audio?
- ☐ Plenty of hospitality ideas?
- ☐ Sharing the home?
- ☐ Checked the addresses/contacts at the back of this book?

6
Community Involvement

Many retired people would like to do something useful for society now that they are free to choose where their real interests lie. Of course, during all our normal working lives we do make a contribution to the welfare of society and the creation of wealth, but there is something about the *voluntary* nature of social involvement that is specially attractive to many people. Often they are pleased at the chance to become more fully involved in a particular cause, or new area of involvement.

Widest variety of opportunity

There is virtually no limit to how one can serve community interests, from spending a few hours a week with some charitable organisation to practically full-time work for a social agency. Just as there are opportunities for voluntary service overseas (VSO) for young people before they take up full-time employment, so there are opportunities for overseas service for qualified technicians in developing countries. Some people, particularly those who retire early, offer their technical and business skills in countries where there is a special need.

So in considering voluntary or paid **community service** there are more opportunities than there ever were when one first began work. Most voluntary organisations have only a small full-time staff, and depend very much on volunteers and part-timers. This means that working relationships are different from those in commercial organisations, and values may be different. In some ways they may seem more casual and less efficient, but one should not judge them by commercial criteria. The people who work with them do so for different reasons and with different objectives, both personal and organisational. One should not join them expecting to lick them into shape with professional expertise; they must be joined with commitment to the *cause,* not business efficiency. Because salaries are small or non-existent many voluntary bodies offer modest expenses (this is certainly so with overseas work). But many retired people take part in community service for free, simply because they enjoy the work.

Considerations in making choices

Perhaps the first thing when considering voluntary or community service is to accept that it is *not* the same as a hobby or home interest. Service involves a **commitment** coupled with a **professional attitude.** Many community activities possible in retirement were also possible during one's working life but they are to be undertaken no less seriously for that. Prison visiting, for example, requires a firm commitment. If a visitor is casual about visits to 'clients' no useful relationship can be built up, and the prisoner may feel more let down than if he/she had no visitor at all. The point is that community service does involve helping people and one should not play fast and loose with human beings. Retired people who are just looking for something different or unusual to do should not consider community service.

Politics

Few people become interested in party politics suddenly and join a political party for the first time on retirement. But many people have belonged to political parties and political clubs before, and know how important volunteer workers are. There is always a demand for help, from delivering leaflets and editing newsletters to acting as branch secretary or treasurer. Political parties rely heavily on members' *enthusiasm* because all their activities are partisan — not everyone in the community at large will agree with their ideology or policy.

Older people who are moderate in their views can have an important *mediating influence* in politics, helping to shift the balance towards community consensus and away from doctrinaire enthusiasm. Some older people have not lost their early fire and are only too delighted to plunge themselves into the hurleyburley of confrontational politics. Perhaps involvement in party politics is the least popular interest among retired people, but that may itself be a good reason for considering it. It is undoubtedly a pity that party politics tend to be looked down on; if more older people were to be involved perhaps the reputation of politics would improve.

"I thought they were supposed to be the silent majority!"

Perhaps more popular than party politics are action and **pressure groups** like CND or women's groups. There is no end to such a list. Many of these groups appeal particularly to young people but the interest and support of older people can be a real asset. Sometimes older people sustain their interest over a longer period than youngsters, who may drop out. Retired people are increasingly visible in all sorts of public demonstrations — for peace, animal rights, prisoners of conscience, community development, law and order issues and so on. They also make up a large proportion of flag-sellers and those who help with street collections. Perhaps they have more confidence than young people; perhaps long experience leads them to appreciate how important some causes are.

Retired people might like to consider standing for election as **local councillors;** they are well placed to give their time to civic duties and have more spare time to deal with the electorate than councillors with jobs to do. At parish council level the duties are less demanding; there are often no party political affiliations, so one can stand as an independent candidate (and stand a very good chance of election in some areas). Parish council work can be just sufficiently demanding without being too onerous for people who still need flexibility in their week. And by entering politics one can combine a special interest with a more public one.

Church work

Church congregations tend to be made up of older people, though youth organisations have always been strong in the churches. There are plentiful opportunities for social involvement and probably more variety for each individual than can be found in other kinds of organisation. One can be involved with a number of different projects and with contrasting groups of people. Churches often have a *family* atmosphere which many maturer people find inviting. If you belong to a church you can help a little with many things and do not have to be so committed as with a single-issue organisation. There is probably more purely social activity with a church than with other organisations.

Some kinds of activity seem to fit church life better than other organisations. Anglican churches have a well organised interest in flower arrangement with some superb flower festivals; but they also offer unique opportunities for needlework and music. Joining a church choir can be more relaxing than a choral society and for many singers just as satisfying; the choral repertoire of Anglican churches is likely to be different from that of non-conformist and Catholic churches.

Some retired people actually seek ordination to a **mature ministry** while others undertake lay duties, sometimes taking on full responsibility for a church or congregation without a full time minister. Some people even join a religious order on retirement.

Youth organisations

Running a youth club is essentially a job for young people but that does not mean that older people cannot make a useful contribution especially when they have real skills to offer. Sports coaching is one area where former games players can help; indeed there is not a single sporting or outdoor activity where an older person does not have something valuable to offer. Some youth work can be done in church organisations, the YMCA or YWCA but many local authority and voluntary youth clubs welcome the interest, support and practical help of older people. Retired people often get on much better with teenagers than younger adults. Inviting youngsters into a mature home can be a productive social experience on both sides. Although they may not admit it, many young people need the company of adults outside their own family and find it easier to relate to people who are not in their own family or family circle.

Old people's organisations

We do not all grow old at the same pace or enjoy the same quality of health. Some people of early retirement age are not active and may be in need of much help. Of course, very old people need help too, but here again age is no indicator of physical or emotional health. A lot of help given *to* the elderly is given *by* the elderly, and retired people often want to help older people while in the early days of their own retirement. Perhaps a contemporary of one's own has become incapacitated or a relative is hospitalised and needs to be regularly visited.

There is no end of opportunities for voluntary work in hospitals and homes. Young people are always welcome in hospital, but often it is only older people who have the maturity of experience to offer real comfort. This may be especially so with hospices for the terminally ill; older people usually have the depth of understanding to be sympathetic and optimistic.

Life can be very lonely for anyone at any age but in sickness it can seem worse. Retired people often have the patience as well as the time to be able to listen to people without criticism, and can devote the time to come back again that sick and lonely people need so much.

The **WRVS** (Women's Royal Voluntary Service) provides opportunities for various kinds of voluntary service including the meals-on-wheels service. They also need help in crisis situations, and people who have cars or can drive can be invaluable if they will undertake emergency duties. The various Friends of Hospital organisations also need help; Hospital Radio may appeal to some who can make themselves available during the normal working day or at weekends.

Theatres

There are many amateur and repertory theatres up and down the country. All of them use volunteers in some way. Box office staff in amateur theatres are invariably volunteers. There is usually a rich social life around the theatre as well as a chance to work backstage. Even municipal theatres can use volunteers.

Stately homes, museums and shows
Stately homes need **stewards** to be in attendance and there are often keen volunteers as well as estate staff. The National Trust is actually a voluntary organisation; although it employs a large number of professional workers there are frequent opportunities to help out as stewards in great houses open to the public and as assistants in the National Trust shops. Some museums need **guides,** voluntary or paid part time, and there is an occasional demand for assistance with the great flower shows and county shows held throughout the summer.

Advice-giving bodies
There is an ever-increasing number of bodies offering advice and counselling to various sectors of the public. There is always a shortage of volunteers and the jobs all demand some training and a fair amount of commitment. The **Citizens Advice Bureaux** recruit advisory staff and deal with a vast range of problems. As well as being trained one has to be able to handle official and technical data, and be sympathetic to clients who may want a simple answer to a problem that is legally very complicated. Counsellors working for the **Samaritans** are also trained and carefully selected but the work is emotionally very demanding because one is often dealing with the raw frontiers of desperation and threatened suicide.

Some people undertake **Marriage Guidance** and related areas, but counsellors are chosen according to special criteria and the training is fairly arduous. Marriage guidance counsellors are mostly below retirement age but retired people may get a chance to help out in administrative jobs (secretary to a branch, committee member, telephone duty).

There are endless other specialist counselling organisations for matters such as alcoholism (Alcoholics Anonymous), gambling, drug taking, AIDS, Multiple Sclerosis, Anorexia and almost every disease with long term effects. These jobs are all emotionally very demanding and may only appeal if one has some personal experience of such ailments and so is deeply committed. But they are all tremendously worthwhile and any retired person could well consider offering some support for one or other of these charities, if only to express thanks for one's own healthy and successful life and retirement.

Schools
In the past schools have shown little interest in drawing on help from the

community, but the situation is changing. With greater involvement of parents in the government of schools there is certain to be an increase in community interest. Some schools do very much welcome help from members of the community (indeed, Community Schools are organised for this very purpose). Many primary schools welcome help in building equipment and helping to look after children, including hearing them read. Secondary schools certainly could use much more of the expertise available in the community than they often do, and it is well worth contacting the local Head to see what you might do to help. It is best to go with some positive but open ideas as to what you might do in the spirit of *offering* the skills you earned your living by. Almost certainly there will be something you can do, even if it is just talking to a group of students considering working in the same kind of job as yourself.

There really is no limit to the amount and variety of community service available. However, one does need the right disposition and the right attitude to it; it tends to involve high **commitment** because people will come to depend on your help in ways that are not easily curtailed. For instance, any form of visiting must be sustained because the person(s) visited come to depend on you and will be exceedingly disappointed, if not inconvenienced, if you do not turn up. On the other hand people who volunteer to be available as required can serve a valuable need by being an extra resource that helps some enterprise to survive.

Checklist
Community Involvement

☐   Right attitude and commitment for voluntary work?
☐   Take part in public/local political life?
☐   Opportunities to play a part in the local church?
☐   Work with young people?
☐   Work with the elderly?
☐   Advisory and counselling opportunities?
☐   Helping a local school?
☐   Talked over options with family and friends?
☐   Ready to take the plunge?
☐   Checked the addresses/contacts at the back of this book?

7
Hobbies and Interests

For many people contemplating retirement the most pleasurable prospect is the chance to enjoy greater **leisure.** Somehow most of us feel that in our working life there is never enough leisure time and we look forward to a time when we can please ourselves. Perhaps this says more about the way work now dominates our economic world than about the nature of retirement. After all, in medieval times over half the days in the year were dedicated to a 'holyday' of some kind, and the blend between work and leisure may well have been more satisfactory.

There does seem to be a basic problem about dividing our time into work (which is in some way disagreeable) and leisure (which is supposed to be wholly agreeable). The fact is that both work *and* non-work are agreeable *and* disagreeable in turns; in retirement we will still find that some things we become committed to can be just as irksome as anything in full-time work.

But as we move into retirement we have expanded opportunities to do what we choose: there will be plenty of time to discover whether we do actually want to classify all those postage stamps we have accumulated over the last three decades.

The idea of hobbies
The idea of hobbies is a strange one. Hobbies are not sports or games but mental or practical interests that are somehow thought to be *improving* in the Victorian sense. There is often felt to be something not quite respectable about having a hobby as an adult — hobbies are supposed to be something little boys and girls do in order to occupy their time usefully. But all adults have some interests that they have pursued with greater or lesser enthusiasm in life, even if they do just see them as hobbies. They are the ways in which one fills one's leisure time when left alone to do as one wishes. So we bring these into our retirement as personal resources and sometimes rush straight into them to break the boredom that soon falls on those who have too much leisure.

For some people retirement certainly is an opportunity to spend greater time on a long-established hobby and perhaps in bringing a long-standing project to completion. These are the **residual interests** of our working life that may or may not serve us in good stead. Paradoxically, one of the attractions of the hobby may have been that it could *not* be fulfilled: its very incompleteness was the spur. For most people their hobbies will continue much as before and not take up more of their time; sometimes they will even fall into abeyance. They will serve the same purpose as they did before, of being there for odd moments rather than as a full-time obsession. Indeed, one would not be making good use of retirement by retiring into a hobby to the exclusion of an expanding new lifestyle.

CHOOSING A NEW HOBBY

So for many people it is choosing a **new hobby** that will become important. We may begin to do something we rejected before. But since many hobbies involve some form of collecting or accumulation of materials they will cost money and may not be the kind of investment they would have been if started at the beginning of one's adult life.

The best kind of hobby is one you can pick up and put down at will, one that can be indulged in whenever you feel like doing something on your own or are at a loose end.

Nature and recreation
Bird watching, popular with so many, is a good recreation because there is always something you can do. Even if it is pouring with rain you can count the birds or you can throw out some food scraps and note the order in which the different species arrive. You can study ornithological books and magazines when you can't get out and you can look for birds on even the shortest walks. If you become really keen you can visit bird sanctuaries and look for rare species when their arrival is announced. You can join clubs or informal groups or just go bird-watching on your own. You can watch from indoors through the window anywhere or walk in the country. You can do a little or a lot as the fancy takes you, and enjoy the company of enthusiasts of all ages.

An interest in **wild flowers and trees** can form the basis of a versatile hobby. There are lots of superb books of wild flowers that you can browse through on a rainy day — some secondhand books are collectors' items. There are always flowers to be seen wherever you go, whether in the country, the local park or on a walk to the shops. Again it is an interest shared with many people and even those who have no particular knowledge of flowers will enjoy talking about ones they see in your company and are identified as having a familiar name even if the flower itself is unknown to them. Trees are perhaps more difficult since they change their appearance throughout the year but there are always plenty of trees to identify and there is the added interest of the wood used in manufacture. Could *you* spot whether an antique chair is made of oak, walnut, mahogany or 'fruitwood'? Any hobby connected with the natural world can deepen our understanding of the mysteries of life.

Practical hobbies

The range of practical hobbies is endless, from flower arrangement to repairing things around the house. Some may require new skills but can be done anywhere and at any time — embroidery, knitting, wood carving. Many hobbies can be pursued at an evening or adult education class and some people like to learn a new hobby this way each year — one year pottery, another woodturning or oil painting. You don't have to keep up a hobby for ever, and regular change can almost become a hobby itself.

Other practical classes can be taken at local colleges; most local education authorities publish a brochure or newspaper with all the details at the start of the academic year in August or September. But if your retirement begins later or you develop an interest during the year it is usually possible to join a class later or at the start of a new term. Just phone the college and ask.

Gardening

Gardening must be one of the commonest interests among retired people, either as a hobby or a full-time interest. Even having a window box can provide gardening pleasure because at least three 'shows' are possible with one window box — spring bulbs, summer flowers and autumn foliage. If a single small box can offer this much interest, a small garden can offer endless possibilities.

Most gardeners have been interested in their hobby throughout their lives and are not going to lose their enthusiasm very much. But in retirement there is often more time available and you can get into the garden at the right time so that jobs do not pile up or go by default. This generally means that gardens are more tidily kept and better cared for by retired people. Some even take on one or two neighbours' gardens, at least to cut the grass and keep the weeds down.

As one grows older, some of the jobs in the garden become harder and it then pays to make the garden as self-regulating as possible. The vegetable garden gets smaller, annual flowers are replaced by shrubs, and paving replaces vast expanses of lawn. On the other hand, gardens that need little upkeep can be more interesting throughout the year than ones that require constant attention.

As with other hobbies, gardening provides a lot of incidental interest, such as reading books, visiting garden centres and botanical gardens; there is always conversation to be had since almost everyone has some kind of interest in gardens. But the idea of gardens as an interest for retired people can be over-romanticised. Gardening is not to everyone's taste and such a taste is not suddenly acquired. For many people keeping a garden tidy is just a domestic chore; it is not exactly disagreeable but is more a matter of neighbourliness than enthusiasm. Most people would rather look at a neat and colourful garden than do all the work required!

Cooking

Cooking may have more universal appeal than gardening. Certainly it is one activity that cannot be avoided, though there are no doubt *some* clever souls who manage to get through life without even boiling a kettle. Again, in retirement we probably have more time to devote to cooking or at least the preparation of meals. Cookery classes are usually available at local colleges of Further Education (many of which have Catering Departments) and sometimes at the Adult Education College. One can either learn the basics of cooking or specialist forms such as *cordon bleu* or *nouvelle cuisine* and attending classes can bring new friends.

It is possible to eat remarkably well without elaborate cooking. Cold food is every bit as good for you as hot food, if more boring over time. But most people enjoy food, particularly if it is eaten in company, and like to perfect one or two special dishes. Some meals can be made interesting just by the variety of what is offered. Breakfasts can be made quite exotic just by the way the table is set and the choice of foods on offer. This is why buffets score so well.

Retired people living alone may become careless about their eating and not achieve a **balanced diet.** Care needs to be taken not to fall into slack ways. Eating out does not always provide the variety and balance needed. The best way of ensuring that you eat well, or at least better than you would, is to entertain once a week, or so, even if it is just to invite a friend in for lunch. One advantage is that you invariably over-cater when entertaining so there will be some nutritious leftovers to take you through the next day or two. It also makes shopping more interesting and gradually you learn a few interesting dishes that take no time at all to make.

Cooking, even at its simplest, is a creative act. No two people cook in the same way or prepare quite the same meals. There is always something to be done in the kitchen, and there is always a sense of achievement. Make up your own recipes, but read how other people cook, too. There are lots of cookery books on the market to suit all needs and many of them are very inexpensive — especially those on sale at supermarkets. Even if you can't get straight up and make something without going to the shops first there are preparations to be done that will occupy your time if you are really bored or if you have a drove of guests arriving.

Out of doors

In retirement you probably won't want to take up any new sports. If you have been a regular games player you may have changed your style and games over the years. Perhaps a few people take up golf or bowls on retirement but by and large you don't suddenly become interested in sport just because you have retired. However, some people do take up swimming, some even for the first time.

Yet keeping fit is as important as ever, though few people bother much with their physical condition until it becomes a problem. Many people begin to improve in physical fitness in retirement, when perhaps they should have started earlier. Nevertheless, one of the many positive aspects of retirement is that health can begin to improve after years of sedentary work.

So it is well worth making some effort to make sure you keep fit and are in good physical shape. For this the key requirements are the right **food** and plenty of **exercise**. Both are often neglected by middle-aged people but it is never too late to start an improvement. The best and simplest form of exercise is regular walking. Try to walk at least two miles a day — probably no more than you did while at work. Going shopping every day or collecting the newspaper will help to boost your mileage. So will going to post a letter, especially if you go to a main post office and not just the post box at the end of the street. Walking the dog can help (so long as it is the right kind of dog!) and a walk round the block on Sundays and holidays or in the evening before turning in can all help to keep the body exercised. The important thing is to be fairly consistent and systematic. Like everything else, walking can be something of a strain when done only occasionally, but when done regularly it becomes no effort at all. You can monitor your fitness by the ease with which you walk up the nearest hilly street.

Why not try a country walk every so often? Once a week would be good, but once a month will do. But beware — country walks do not provide enough exercise if one dawdles. So try to make it a proper country walk, even if it is on the flat, and burn up some energy. Try to find your best pace for walking so that once you start out you don't keep slowing down. There are lots of good books of country walks: try your local bookshop or library. It is a good idea to take a walking companion so that there are two of you to help in making the decision to get out of the car. There is no need to have walking boots for rambles — especially if the idea of changing is a disincentive — good stout shoes will do well enough.

Study

Some retired people like to undertake a course of study in a subject that interests them. There are many ways of doing this from attending at the local **College of Further Education** to taking a **correspondence course** leading to a university degree. Learning a foreign language is popular because you can listen to tapes at home, perhaps when you are on your own, and practise if you go abroad. You can study virtually anything without going too far from home and in many cases win a formal certificate or diploma.

One is never too old to study. People in their late seventies have read for degrees and a study course can enrich the enjoyment of what was just a hobby before. If you want to take an **Open University** degree you can watch programmes at home on television, listen to radio programmes related to the course and join a local study group with fellow students. There is also an OU Summer School and social events for students. There are other qualification-awarding bodies that build on previous qualifications and life experience such as the American Columbia Pacific University; but be a little cautious about the respectability of some of these privately-managed 'award-bestowing' institutions. Get advice if necessary. The reputable ones will be approved by the British Accreditation Council.

Writing

Sometimes people contemplate taking up writing in retirement. If they do they can be sure of two things — they won't write a bestseller and they won't earn a living out of it! One doesn't become a famous writer overnight and if you haven't been a writer during your working life it is unlikely that you will suddenly learn the art after retirement. Most people grossly underestimate the skill needed for professional writing and do not realise how long it takes to get from typescript to publication; and that is without being paid for the work. But everyone probably has one book in them, often an autobiography or a book dealing with their favourite hobby; if you do feel inclined to write, then go ahead!

One of the best ways to test yourself as a writer is to try and write reviews for a local newspaper. These could for example be drama reviews or reports of sporting events. If you can succeed at this it might be worth branching out. Best-selling romantic novels don't come that easily and it could take years for an idea to become commercially publishable. But you might like to take a hand in putting together a local guide book or history book with a group of interested people. If you are really keen to get into print by yourself you might want to finance the book yourself and pay to have it published; but the pitfalls are many (especially marketing and distribution) and you must be prepared to lose your investment.

Entertainment

One great advantage of retirement is that you can go to your favourite forms of entertainment. If you are of pensionable age you will qualify for **pensioners' reductions** even if it means going to matinees and first houses. But it is worth trying to make use of such advantages to extend your familiarity with your favourite art form — music, drama, opera, cinema or whatever.

Retired people often ignore the opportunity for an extended cultural life, contenting themselves with a surprisingly low level of social involvement. It is only too easy to accept second rate standards once one is retired and a measure of one's standards is the quality of cultural life one maintains.

Checklist
Hobbies and Interests

- ☐ Long-standing leisure interests?
- ☐ Discovering new interests?
- ☐ Links with outdoor life/the natural world?
- ☐ Explore possible evening classes to gain new skills and enjoy new company?
- ☐ Gardening — joy or chore?
- ☐ Cooking — new creative opportunities?
- ☐ Fitness and exercise?
- ☐ Being a 'mature student'?
- ☐ Discovering yourself as a writer?
- ☐ Taking advantage of special reductions and discounts?
- ☐ Checked the addresses/contacts at the back of this book?

8
Business Venturing

Retired people who have worked for someone else all their lives often fancy the idea of going into business for themselves in a small way, especially if they retire quite early, say before the age of fifty-five. If you have been working for yourself or owned a business it is natural to want to maintain such an interest. It is certainly good to see retirement as the chance for a fresh start but it is unwise to take on too much, especially so far as risking capital is concerned.

Self-employed versus working for someone else
For most people it is better to work for someone else rather than be self-employed in retirement. Starting up a business is by no means easy and many if not most new businesses fail within a year of being set up. Even those who have run a successful business often don't succeed in a new sphere of trading. If you do go into business on your own, do it in a small way with the minimum capital investment and risk.

If you do really want to have a shot at surviving in business it is best to lay the foundations several years before retirement. This way you will have some idea of what is involved and be able to get the business turning over before you depend on it for income. You may not be able to spend much time with your business while doing a full-time job, but perhaps your spouse or a relative or even a retired friend can help you build it up, providing support until you can become more fully involved yourself.

As any accountant or bank manager could tell you, very few businesses show whether they are truly viable or not in under three to five years. Even businesses which do very well in the first year or two may exhaust the market, with the result that liabilities increase. Be very wary of 'instant' businesses of the sort that are advertised from time to time. They are often fads and even the best ones tend to depend too much on the original entrepreneur who really just wants outlets to expand his own business.

On the other hand, there are many ways of making money provided you already have the right connections and know the business scene well. After all, most younger people go into business because they recognise a particular opportunity. But all businesses require very hard work and dedication. Customers do *not* beat a track to your door brandishing five pound notes just because you have a good idea for making money. As one London accountant put it, 'Ideas are cheap, capital is expensive.'

Part-time work

The best way of increasing your retirement income is to continue in the trade or profession you worked at full time, either by doing some extra part-time work for the company you worked for, or by offering your services to another firm (on the whole it is better for social reasons to choose a new company). Someone who has been an accountant or book-keeper might be able to find part-time work with a small company that needs a little expert help in that field, especially if they cannot afford full-time staff.

Some firms like to take on one or two former employees in a new capacity to help with a project that does not relate to their former job. Welfare work is one example; some retired members of a firm may go back for a year or two to help with different aspects of welfare, say visiting former employees. At other times special projects are set up in a new area, for example a museum or heritage centre. If you work for a large company which has not done something like this, why not suggest it, plan it, and arrange for it to coincide with your retirement?

Sometimes you will find you have certain skills in demand for a few hours a week — not your original professional skills, but something for which you have a facility. You may be able to do secretarial work with your home computer for a company that needs a little extra secretarial help, even though you never worked as a clerk or secretary. Simple book-keeping or invoicing is another area where many small businesses can do with a couple of hours' help each week. Indeed, many small businesses fail just because there is no one to do the invoicing and statements, and so the cash flow dries up.

Some people like to take a job quite unlike the one they did before, and one that is quite demanding. Office cleaning in its various forms is one example that may appeal to some people. The hours are unsocial but may suit a retired person well. Many of the jobs that students take in vacation time fall into this category and it may even suit you to cox and box over holidays and term-time with a student.

There will always be a number of part-time jobs available if you are not too fussy. A group of you might like to band together to offer a service in your district of doing 'unpopular' jobs. This itself could become a small business involving little capital risk and little expenditure for setting up, other than for the printing of leaflets.

Consultancy

Some professional people — and you must be a professional to do it — set up consultancy services in their particular area of skills. They may compete with other professional companies and take on business commitments using their length of experience as a selling point. It is not unusual for people like policemen and firemen to set up consultancies in their professional area such as crime watch and security, or advising on fire hazards. Being an 'ex' is a positive advantage here. But in almost all other areas there will be customers who want just what you can offer at a fee they can afford. You will not be undercutting the 'big boys', just offering a different service at a different price.

Other forms of consultancy may be developed on a more *ad hoc* basis. For instance, while there may not be a regular demand for advice on garden landscaping or the buying of antiques, from time to time someone may want such help and if the business is set up ready it can trade (and cease to trade) according to demand.

Do take care how you set up your new venture — particularly if you go into legal partnership or form a limited company. No business venture should proceed without **legal advice.** Many an activity entered into with friends in all good faith on both sides turns sour during the course of trading. And there are often implications for **taxation** if you are earning income. Of course, any money that is paid to you for any service or product is of interest to the Inland Revenue. If you are considering undertaking any business enterprise you should first of all talk with your accountant or local tax inspector — this may well be the first time you have ever met the latter.

Retail trading

There are lots of possibilities in retail, especially if you do not need to make a full living out of trading. To some people the idea of a market stall is appealing but unless you have experience of this kind you should avoid it. Successful market traders are very skilled at both buying *and* selling and very few people can learn these skills late in life. But you might like to help on a stall and if you know a trader well they may welcome some part-time help. Of course, if all you want to do is meet people you can set up a stall and just wait and see what happens. Some people find a kiosk at a summer seaside resort to be ideal for this sort of thing.

You may prefer the idea of a small shop or café. These are certainly possibilities but are terribly hard and demanding work. You cannot *make* people come into your shop and buy; you have to know how to attract them either from your window display or by the reputation of the business. Unfortunately reputation comes after cash flow, and rents and other overheads have to be paid whether there is income or not.

There are two golden rules about setting up a shop or restaurant:

● never let anyone else manage your business (so you should try not to employ anyone other than your family)
● never buy a business just because someone is selling it; the commonest reason for selling a business is that it is failing!

If you like the idea of being in business but are not interested in personal financial returns or risks, you might like to run a church or charity stall or even shop. Many charity shops are run by volunteers (though managed by professionals) and there will almost certainly be an opportunity near where you live. There are many other charity businesses from selling sweepstake tickets to Christmas cards. Since the main interest is to meet people, large profits will be less important and it will be easier for the venture to survive.

Successful ventures

Much of this may sound discouraging. The reason for urging so much caution is that when people retire they usually want — and need — *less* responsibility and worry about business, not more; the idea of running a new business is for most people a short-lived pipe dream. But there are imaginative ways of earning extra money, even if very few of them will lead to untold wealth. The secret is to do something you really like, want to continue, and are quite prepared to do for someone else if they will pay you.

If you are very fit and enjoy gardening, there will always be someone who will pay for you to maintain their garden while they are on holiday or abroad. If they can afford an expensive holiday you can feel quite justified in asking a fair wage for the job. Cutting the grass for a sick neighbour is a different matter. Instead of giving surplus plants away you might like to sell them. In some parts of the country, gardeners regularly have a wayside table with produce on it and an 'honesty tin' for payment.

If you enjoy cooking and preparing food you may be able to cater for local people who want parties, weddings or christenings. If you are a good cake-maker you can take orders for special cakes (which cost a lot wherever they are bought) and which give a fair profit even when baked at home. Children's parties offer good scope for catering; you provide all the food and presents and let the parents organise the games. Or you can bake for a local shop or delicatessen.

Some people make and sell floral decorations, either real or artificial. Some will do cleaning and caretaking. House minding while someone is away can produce an income. Sometimes house owners want someone to live in while they are away. Dressmaking and tailoring have traditionally been a home industry and you may want to encourage a few regular customers. It is surprising how often people prefer a neighbour to do a job; they feel they are getting a more personal and reliable service. Shortening or altering men's trousers must be a vast potential cottage industry!

Trading from home

One can use a life-long hobby to trade from home in the articles of your choice. It is surprising how many specialist **mail order firms** are based in someone's back bedroom. Lists and catalogues are easily printed and in specialist subjects (crafts, collecting, gadgets) the grapevine is all that is necessary for finding customers. Obvious articles for trade are the particular specialities in postal items — stamp varieties, special issues, ephemera. You could consider anything collectable but make sure the items are small and the postal costs minimal. Rare and scarce items are the best. Some people trade in antique books or other printed material. This means you can have them about the house and enjoy them yourself before selling them. Indeed, dealers in antique furniture often sell their own furniture, their own home being the shop itself.

You can also act as an **agent,** trading from home on someone else's behalf. Or you can collect the items from the warehouse as they are ordered from you and have them sent off as if they were from home. **Import-Export** agencies work in a similar way and you might consider this kind of business if you are a specialist in the area. The *Exchange & Mart* published each Thursday, is full of such opportunities and contacts.

Tutoring

Even people who have not been teachers can make good tutors if they know their subject well and are able to help others to learn. There are a number of **private tutorial colleges** up and down the country which offer part-time and occasional work to qualified people. Have a look at *Yellow Pages*. It may be that you are a fluent or native speaker in a language that some business executive needs for an overseas visit. Even if you cannot 'teach' them you may be able to offer conversation practice.

How about teaching an evening or afternoon class at your local **College of Adult or Further Education**? Many classes come into being just because there *is* a teacher available. On the whole the demand is for the more unusual and exotic subjects rather than traditional 'school' subjects, so people who have never taught at all may find there is a demand for what they can offer. If you do want to teach for a local education authority you may have to take a special course of training as an adult educator but the authority will pay for this and the experience itself can be great fun.

Could you teach . . .

Antique collecting, bookbinding, crafts, car repair and maintenance, market gardening, modern languages (French, Spanish, German, Italian), metalwork, woodwork, pottery, needlework, French cuisine, cake-making, business management, electronics, local history/archaeology, bird-watching, upholstery, picture restoration . . .?

Of course, there is nothing to stop you setting up your own tutorial school. You only need to be able to attract the customers, and some people have skills that are very much in demand. Many cookery schools start off in this way; lessons in gardening, indoor plant care, flower arrangement, clock making, car maintenance and repair are all possibilities that could be done on a small scale and for a small group of students meeting once a week.

Success in business

Actually, no-one knows how to be successful in business — at least not so they can tell anyone else. There seems to be a certain magic in being successful in business on your own, and even then you need luck and good management. But provided you don't risk any of your capital, it could well be worth having a go at some kind of business venture. Business can be fun, and broaden one's experience of life and of other people. A useful book to read is *How to Raise Business Finance* by Peter Ibbetson (in this same series) filled with valuable information and advice on such topics as raising a bank loan, preparing cash flows, and doing viability forecasts. It covers what to do when things go right, and when things go wrong.

Checklist
Business Venturing

- ☐ Got the right temperament?
- ☐ Got any relevant experience?
- ☐ Properly planned before retirement?
- ☐ Part-time work opportunities?
- ☐ Consultancy work opportunities?
- ☐ Retailing shops, charity shops, market stalls?
- ☐ Sell your services — gardening, cooking, etc?
- ☐ Trading from home by mail order? Import/Export?
- ☐ Tutoring or teaching? Special skills or experience to offer?
- ☐ Fully prepared? Able to take the risk?
- ☐ Taken professional advice?
- ☐ Understand the importance of sales and marketing?
- ☐ Checked the addresses/contacts at the back of this book?

9
Family and Friends

One of the joys of prospective retirement is the possibility of being able to visit friends and family who live away from home. When family members live overseas it is tempting to arrange to visit them for a period of time and perhaps see grandchildren for the first time. Visiting old friends, too, may now become possible with cheap flights to exotic places. For other people, being able to spend more time at greater leisure with family and friends in the UK will be one of the exciting prospects of retirement.

While these new opportunities are important, it is also worthwhile making sure they are successful; if not properly planned or rightly judged they can sometime lead to a good deal of disappointment. On the other hand, with careful and sensible planning, they can be the experiences of a lifetime.

Travel overseas
Some aspects of planning a visit to friends and family overseas may not be entirely obvious, especially if the times of the visit are determined by you and not your hosts. For one thing, visits to the southern hemisphere will be to a 'reversed season'. Melbourne, for example can be too cold and wet in their winter and too hot and steamy in their summer. Sydney can be unbearable with heat in their summer. Spring in the Canadian prairies can be plagued by black fly, and summer in the southern United States can be harshly hot. In other words you may find the climate far from your liking and there is little you can do about it once you have arrived; going elsewhere may be impossible.

Do be sure that you have plenty of accessible funds, not only in case of emergencies but in case additional travel opportunities arise that are too good to miss. Never rely *too* much on all your 'extra' expenses being covered, even by the children. They will have financial commitments of their own but may not want to seem mean with parents and relatives. Make sure you are adequately insured, especially against sickness.

Changed lifestyles

More than this, the lifestyles of people you have known at home may be very different in their new homeland. Grandparents can be quite upset by the social habits of their grandchildren and may find they are less well regarded than by other grandchildren back home. Friends with whom you had great times in younger days may have grown into a quite unfamiliar way of life. Elderly Brits do not even wear the same kinds of clothes that their contemporaries wear overseas.

So it is important to do a good deal of planning and research before visiting even people you know. Do your homework thoroughly and assess the situation; don't rely on an 'open' invitation especially when *you* have engineered it! Living with people for several weeks, however well you have once known them, is very different in a foreign country from back home. There are no easy excuses for a sudden return home especially when you have bought a ticket on a charter or APEX flight.

On the other hand, with the right preparations, you can have the time of your life. Why not put into your itinerary some flexible time that you organise yourself? Stop off for a few nights somewhere en route; organise a local holiday of your own. And make sure you have plenty of spending money so that you can do more than pay your own way. Part of planning an overseas visit should be to include the chance of something you have never done before. Careful reading about places on a possible route will open up possibilities and you may be able to visit family and friends in several places. Check out your local library, travel agents, and the national tourist offices or embassies, and collect plenty of brochures and information.

Living abroad

There can be quite a temptation to go and live with a member of the family who lives abroad. Sometimes a first visit is made which goes really well, and it is felt that permanent residence is a possibility. This is very seldom the case. Most families can cope with short family visits of say up to three weeks. Most families abroad can cope with even an annual visit of short-ish duration. But few families can stand the strain of parents for several months on end, especially as they grow older.

One of the reasons for this is that none of us can slip into a new culture as if we had always known it. Even Canada and Australia are much more different from home than many elderly people will admit to themselves. Visitors can get irritated by matters that the natives take for granted, for they will never be treated as they were at home.

Overseas monetary values

For example, monetary values are quite different overseas. People spend money differently, and have different attitudes towards it. If you think of all the elderly immigrants at home — of any nationality at all — you will have some idea of how *you* will seem, even in an old Commonwealth country.

And money can become a problem if you have not arranged it in the right places. For instance, you can draw your State Retirement Pension almost anywhere in the world, but if you live outside the EEC it remains at the nominal value of the day you left home. This means you could start to become a financial drain on your family abroad.

Visiting family in the UK

Similar considerations apply here. Will you be visiting family outside their holiday periods? If so they can leave you to your own devices and you can spend the day at your own pace. You may also be able to do some of the little jobs that need doing, and help out with some of the big ones. You can babysit while the parents get out for once in a while, and you can take grandchildren on excursions and give their parents some time together.

But suppose you chose the wrong time for your visit, or used up their valuable vacation time they would have spent differently? You may unwittingly outstay your welcome, and not be given any sign that this was so. You may cause expense that can be ill-afforded or find yourself committed to doing things you would not normally do or cannot afford.

On the other hand, it would be foolish never to visit friends or family just in case they are inconvenienced. Visits from grandparents are almost invariably welcomed and some can be nicely timed to benefit everyone. Staying over a bank holiday can be a good way of turning a dreary time into one with lots of activity, albeit of a very local kind not far from the home.

Having visitors

Retirement is also a time to enjoy one's own home and to play host to family and friends. Instead of having to cram all your invitations into a couple of weeks in the year you can spread them more conveniently.

Having guests for the weekend or just overnight is very pleasurable. Grandchildren will enjoy a night or two with their grandparents but may have to be specially invited as their parents may not want them to be a nuisance. Providing a home-from-home to growing grandchildren can be enormously beneficial. Most youngsters get on better with their grandparents than their parents, particularly during adolescence. But don't expect too much *from* them. Take them as they are and don't expect them to be perfect angels. Indeed it is precisely because they are not 'perfect' that they need the love and affection of grandparents.

Correspondence

If you enjoy letter writing, retirement is the time to cultivate it. As people get older they tend to lose touch with old friends, often with regret. Letter writers are important people in social organisation; they hold the world together. Letters do not have to be long or confined to Christmas. Birthday cards with a few scribbled words keep friendships alive for decades. Picture postcards can be sent from time to time either while on holiday or from a stock collected specially for the purpose. Correspondence is often one-sided and you must not be pertubed if you get fewer letters and cards than you send; your letters are nonetheless appreciated.

Keeping up friendships

Indeed, one of the realities of most relationships is that they *are* one-sided. Never get distressed because no one calls or writes or telephones. Most people — sad to say — allow relationships to fade without effort to maintain them. But when someone takes the trouble to get in touch the response is usually immediate. Some of us are initiators, most of us are responders. Never be afraid to open up a friendship by offering an invitation. Rather than *expect* people to visit you, why not call and *invite* people into your own home?

Friendships are always precious and old ones have a special quality that is often slow to grow with new ones. But we need both kinds; the old ones to sustain and the new ones to stimulate. Friendships don't just happen — they develop, and only do so with attention and effort. They grow and flourish in their own time and cannot be rushed, but they are also slow to wither and surprisingly hardy; often totally indestructible.

Good friendships can be better than many family relationships and for this reason alone we should not confine our social life to our families. Family relationships do not provide us with that freedom and flexibility we need to flourish and be ourselves. Desirable though good family relationships may be, they cannot cope with all the needs of life and are put under too much strain when more is expected of them than they can sustain. The reality is that for a good many people family relations have become strained or impoverished. We cannot expect a warm, loving family to surround us suddenly at the age of sixty if things have been very different in the past.

Single people

Retired people may live alone; indeed, statistically more than half of all retired people will do so eventually. Family and friends become even more important in such cases but the flexibility that has to be shown is greater than ever, for the most positive of reasons. One parent or friend can usually be accommodated at home more easily than two (or four) so there will be more opportunity for going away to stay. But you may also feel more often in need of company and will have to invite people very deliberately and with plenty of preparation.

It is probably easier for a single person to take a lodger or occasional paying guest. A student can bring a breath of fresh air into the house and a young relative might be a good choice. A friend or relative who visits your town on an occasional or even regular basis may welcome the offer of accommodation. If you need company there are plenty of ways of obtaining it. Actors, for instance, are often in need of a few nights' stay of the sort that older people (who do not mind late nights) might appreciate.

Social life

Retired people need active social lives both for company and stimulation. Since you don't have to keep regular hours, you can easily fall into slack ways. Really you need more social opportunities than you can make use of. In retirement areas like the seaside resorts there are usually plenty of things to do because the visitors need entertainment. Some resorts cater especially for the retired, particularly out of season. But you should avoid enjoying *only* the company of your own age group. You need younger company, too.

Even if you are not a 'drinker' a decent local pub can be a good place to make casual friends. Pubs do not generally provide close friendships, but they can provide the regular *bonhomie* that older people need. Plenty of people are satisfied with lively conversation in the pub or club, without expecting any greater personal involvement. If you want more intimate relationships, of course, they can be fostered.

Independent lifestyle

For very few people does their adult lifestyle remain unchanged. Often we recognise critical periods in our life when significant changes occurred. Perhaps we were frequent churchgoers and stopped going for some reason. Perhaps we took an interest in politics in our fifties which changed our whole range of friends. Such changes do not cease at retirement; most people can expect important changes that will significantly alter their personal values and hence the things they do.

This is why it's such a mistake to look on retirement as just a time to catch up on what has been missed or postponed. Your relationships with friends and family will be changing just as your family and friends will be changing their life patterns. And it is not just what you do that will change, but what you *believe*. Retired people with really active minds and social awareness often discover new challenges they would never have imagined a dozen years before.

We should not underestimate such changes in later life. Many people over fifty-five become divorced; some face up to a new sexual orientation; some plunge into a whole new life of service, or indulgence; some are glad to be rid of all family connections and responsibilities; some sell up and go abroad to live in a style they have never been able to experience before; many become aware of themselves for the first time as real individuals. There are many forms of change and it is wrong to see retirement simply as the threshold to old age and a period of social decline and increased family dependency.

Checklist
Family and Friends

- ☐ Overseas trips — properly thought through and planned?
- ☐ Living abroad — aware of the temptations and traps?
- ☐ Sympathetic to the needs of family and friends?
- ☐ Ready to take initiatives yourself — inviting guests, keeping up correspondence, maintaining friendships?
- ☐ Building up a full social calendar?
- ☐ Maintaining an independent lifestyle?
- ☐ Checked the addresses/contacts at the back of this book?

10
Health and Fitness

Good health and fitness come from an attitude of mind. Indeed, people who are active in sports and games may not be as fit and healthy as the less strenuously active, because of past injuries. In later years these may engender health problems, especially if one has not matched sporting interests with a healthy lifestyle. And a healthy lifestyle springs from the way we look upon our world.

Lifestyle

There is no doubt that some people live in a more healthy way than others. Of course, some people seem to be naturally fitter and healthier because their metabolism works that in that way, but most of us do have to work at healthy living. Keeping healthy can be quite difficult if we have not adopted healthy habits over the years — but it really is never too late to start.

The starting point for healthy living is our **attitude to life** and the events that surround us. It is not so much a matter of being generally optimistic, as being realistic. A realistic view of life leads us to look positively at anything that happens to us so that we can draw out of it something advantageous. It means looking for the good in every situation and taking a keen interest in the world around us.

A healthy lifestyle needs us to be moderately busy; always having something to look forward to but never being too pushed for time. It means that we have a future orientation in our life so that we do not have 'empty spaces' to distress or bore us. It means taking charge of our activities and interests so that there is always something pleasant and agreeable ahead. And it means looking positively to engage in physical activity in preference to a sedentary existence.

Using a diary

Keeping a diary is a good way of ensuring our time is planned to cope with what we need to initiate for ourself and with what other people are likely to want of us.

- It means having time free for unexpected invitations and last-minute opportunities
- It means anticipating those times when we get depressed or frustrated because there is nothing to do
- It means making sure we are not over-burdened with things to do and not left with long gaps of time to fill in

For many people Sundays and bank holidays are the times they are most unstimulated and for which they wish they had made previous arrangements. The best way of dealing with such occasions is to invite someone to join you — a member of the family or friends you may not have seen for a while. On these occasions, how about inviting people to join you rather than seeking out invitations to stay with them? You can feel more hurt if a hoped-for invitation is not forthcoming, than if your own invitation is declined!

It always pays to take the initiative rather than wait for someone else to invite you. In this way *you* can decide what *you* want to do. Bank holidays and Sundays are good times socially for exercise and fresh air. There is no need to go shopping or to business but you can go for walks, and probably at greater leisure than during the week. However, some people prefer a regular mid-week excursion so as to avoid the crowds.

A diary is a way, too, of making sure that exercise is well-spaced and placed. You can 'book in' your favourite form of exercise with the regularity you need for continued enjoyment. By using a diary you can make sure you have company when you wish to engage in your favourite sport or leisure activity.

Medical check up

Many people take the opportunity of having a thorough medical check up at their retirement. Some local authorities offer special facilities for this and, of course, your own general practitioner will arrange any kind of medical check up you require. Many employers — especially larger companies — will arrange medical check ups as part of their pre-retirement programmes.

If you belong to a private medical scheme (eg BUPA, PPP) you can also arrange a check up through a private clinic. Private facilities are available specially for this purpose even to those who are not members of schemes.

Also, why not review your normal daily routines to ensure that you are using a healthy regime? Check your eating habits and review your daily ration of exercise. Visit an osteopath or adviser in posture and check that

How fit are you?

		Answer	
Do you quickly get out of breath walking uphill or even on the flat?		☐ Yes	☐ No
Do your legs ache or feel weak after you have climbed a couple of flights of stairs?		☐ Yes	☐ No
Do you find it difficult to bend down and tie your shoe laces or put your socks or tights on?		☐ Yes	☐ No
Do you find it difficult to comb the back of your hair or pull a jumper off?		☐ Yes	☐ No
Is it difficult for you to get out of an arm-chair or the bath?		☐ Yes	☐ No

you have good sitting and standing habits. Make sure that your favourite chair gives you the support you need. Retirement can also be a good time to buy a new bed.

Relaxation

Relaxation is as important as exercise; indeed the two go hand in hand. Make sure that you have plenty of opportunity for relaxation and that you have your own 'tricks' of relaxation. Here are some:

- supply of unread books and magazines
- someone to swap reading materials with
- keep handy a supply of local *What's On* literature
- have some favourite strolls for evenings or Sunday afternoons
- keep by something to be done in the potting shed or garage for a rainy day
- a supply of tapes and records to listen to
- a collection to work on
- letter writing

Sleep

Older people often find they sleep less well than when they were younger. Often they need less sleep. But one still needs to have *enough* sleep. How do *you* prepare yourself for bedtime? What sorts of things help you to sleep well? Try to develop a routine, but with variations.

How do you prepare for sleep?	
☐ read	☐ put the cat out
☐ go for a short walk	☐ take the dog for a walk
☐ have a hot or cold drink	☐ wash the dishes
☐ watch television	☐ ....
☐ listen to the radio	☐ ....
☐ listen to music	☐ ....
☐ pray or meditate	☐ ....
☐ do some physical exercises	☐ ....
	☐ ....

If you wake up in the night, rather than lie there restless you could get up, make yourself a drink, listen to the radio, look out of the window, read, water the plants, do a job about the house, or whatever. Remember, you do not necessarily need to have a full night's sleep; and taking a nap in the afternoon or mid-evening may be a good way of getting the rest you need.

Sports
Older people often continue with sports they played when younger but some sports cannot be played much past the age of 50. Of course, some games can be continued indefinitely — badminton, for example. But the best activities can be continued almost without intermission — walking, cycling, rowing, swimming, even tennis. Other activities like digging and some forms of housework are as good for stamina, suppleness and strength as any energetic sport of younger years.

If you have belonged to a sports club you may want to continue your membership; you may also want to join a health club where you can obtain expert advice and develop a personal fitness programme. Most towns have at least one commercial health club and larger towns have municipal sports centres usually with a fitness gym. The facilities in some of the newer purpose-built ones are superb.

Exercises
Physical exercises for their own sake can be very boring but many people as they get older find they do like to do a few 'physical jerks' from time to time. It seems that as our bodies become less supple, we find the need to restore that suppleness, and doing a series of exercises early in the morning or late at night can be stimulating.

Whatever we do, we should be careful not to cause undue strain. Ideally we should start under instruction or with a book of exercises designed specially for older readers. We need to be gentle and build up progressively over several weeks. A good time to start is on holiday or somewhere away from home so that we can break into a new routine.

Four golden rules of exercise

1   Get moving
2   Build up gradually
3   Exercise regularly
4   Keep it up

Try to choose activities which

● you enjoy
● make you feel good
● you can do for 20 or 30 minutes two or three times a week
● you can fit easily into your everyday routine
● you can do near home
● don't depend on the weather or seasons
● suit your particular fitness needs

Dancing

Various forms of dancing are accessible to retired people. Ballroom dancing is very popular in some areas and there are ballroom dancing clubs in most towns. There are also country and Scottish dancing societies that always welcome new members. It's never too late to take up dancing.

Even if you don't join a club, you can find places where dancing is offered — such as hotels which hold regular or occasional dinner dances, or clubs that organise social events. It is always possible to find a partner even if you live alone; women may be in a majority so men can usually find a partner. Women often dance together when men are not available. If you are very (or even reasonably) energetic you can go to a disco where it does not much matter who you dance with or how well you dance.

Diet and food

Eating good food and having a balanced diet is at least as important in retirement as in earlier years. Check your eating habits and get rid of the bad ones. Eat plenty of fresh food, including fruit and vegetables. And you can cut down on foods that are just stodgy or junk — perhaps the kind of foods you had as a quick snack in a hurried lunchtime while working.

Many people use the opportunity of retirement to take a greater interest in their food and many take up cooking more seriously than previously.

Interesting meals can be prepared with very little cooking, and those living alone can enjoy a great variety. For something special you can always invite someone to share your table.

It is better to eat little and often than to have one binge a day. Try to fit eating in with your exercise and your daily (varied) pattern of activity. Try to make every day a little bit different and to relate your food to your exercise — a light salad before a long walk; some hot soup afterwards; sandwiches and a thermos of soup on a ramble; tea and scones for afternoon; pizza and salad for supper.

Take an interest in food and its preparation and explore different kinds of food shops. Try out unfamiliar vegetables and fruit in the larger supermarkets and get into the habit of keeping your fridge stocked with essential ingredients. Use herbs to give flavour and interest to otherwise simple dishes.

How about checking over your old eating and drinking habits, and seeing what you ought to cut out or cut down? Don't let your consumption of alcohol or tobacco increase — cut out smoking if you can; you should be under less strain anyway. Try new drinks like the herb teas and fruit juice mixes; take a serious interest in wine, and drink carefully — and knowledgeably! Could *you* tell the difference between a claret and a burgundy?

Personal hygiene
There is no reason why we should be less careful with our bodies just because we are older. We should be no less self-aware of our bodily functions than we were as teenagers. Since we have more time we can spend longer on body maintenance.

Regular bathing or showering pays dividends; so does hair care. We might start to go regularly to a chiropodist and manicurist. We could start visiting a sauna and a physiotherapist. Occasional skin treatment is as valuable for men as women — men often need attention to their eyebrows, finger nails, ears.

Perfume and make up are important to women but need to be used properly and subtly. Some older women turn themselves into painted dolls; some older men look as if they have suffered a lifetime of neglect! But men need to look after themselves just as well as women; aftershave and cologne are just as necessary as when the users were 25 (some would say more so!) and their hair will need more attention.

Clothes must be clean, too. Older people can become careless about their clothes and tend to wear them for longer because they are less fashion-conscious. Old and dirty clothes can be unhealthy; all clothes should be cleaned with some frequency. Socks, stockings and underclothes need to be changed regularly (sometimes twice daily) and kept fresh. Many older people become more fastidious about themselves than they ever were when youngsters.

Health and vitality

For many older people, retirement is the healthiest time of their lives because they have more opportunity to look after themselves and, in some cases, more money for personal indulgence. Older people take as much pride in their appearance as young people and often have more encouragement and incentive. But looking good is a consequence of three activities being properly blended:

- thinking well of oneself
- eating well
- exercising well.

There is no need why any retired person should not feel as fit and energetic as they ever did. Not to enjoy retirement is too often only a consequence of an attitude and frame of mind rather than of physical and material disadvantage. More than anything else, good health is something we create for ourselves and we all have the power to look after ourselves as well as we shall ever need.

	Checklist Health and Fitness
☐	Positive attitude to enjoying life?
☐	Keeping busy on a whole range of things?
☐	Keeping a diary to plan the best use of time?
☐	Assessed your own level of fitness?
☐	Medical and dental check-ups?
☐	Following a good physical regime — sleep, diet, exercise?
☐	Getting plenty of varied relaxation?
☐	Belong to a sports club or health club? Swimming?
☐	Dancing?
☐	Body care and maintenance well in hand?
☐	Checked the addresses/contacts at the back of this book?

11
Growing Older

However we may look on retirement, we are entering another transitional period in our life. While we are retired we shall grow perceptibly older and eventually enter the venerable state of old age.

Some people fear this eventual state, but there is no need to. We all of us have an inbuilt mental facility to react to changes in our physical functions and capabilities, and there is no reason why old age should not be as enjoyable as any other stage in our life. Most old people are no worse off in any respect than when they were younger; perhaps they just become more self-preoccupied.

Many people wrongly assume that they will be less well, less healthy, in old age than in youth. Of course, we all suffer from ailments of one kind or another, but one's general disposition and outlook on life may well become *healthier*. Many of our physical complaints will have appeared gradually, some of them traceable back to much earlier years. But later in life one can cosset oneself and enjoy having reasons for not going out in the cold, or for not doing much when the weather is poor.

Slowing down
Most of us have been trying to slow down — usually without success — since we were teenagers. Often we never succeed while in full-time employment, and resist a slower pace even in retirement. But one of the joys of being older is being able to choose our own pace of doing things, without feeling beholden to other people. In later years we can indulge ourself more than ever and make things happen as *we* would wish.

Although our bodies may slow down, our minds can be as bright as ever. We may wonder if our brains are as active as they were, but probably we are just viewing things in a new perspective rather than becoming less mentally able.

Oddly, perhaps, many older people live up to younger people's expectation that they are less able than they were. Some, let it be admitted, actively relish being dependent on others and having people run around for them. And let's remember that there are many young people, more physically handicapped than most old people, who still enjoy full and active lives.

Comfort

Physical comfort matters more as we grow older. That is why many people prefer to move to smaller houses. We should certainly prepare for later years by making sure the home we live in is convenient for us and that friends or relatives are nearby. **Sheltered housing** is a possibility for some people.

We also need spiritual and cultural comforts as well as physical ones; contacts with the local church, chapel, synagogue or mosque could be valuable. At home we need access to radio, television, library books and records; and whatever materials we need for our hobbies.

It is important not to become cut off from people, especially those younger than oneself. If we have been used to making friends among our contemporaries, we need to cultivate younger friends. We have a lot to offer them and they have much to offer us. Grandchildren may be more responsive than our own children — let's try to make plenty of time for them!

Continuing adventures

Life is a unique adventure, and it is good to feel it will continue to be so after retirement. In later years we may have to use a little more imagination to make things happen but we can always do something, even vicariously. We can take an interest in other people around us; we can correspond with people or exchange tapes; we can write to authors whose work we enjoy, and we can make contacts with people working in exciting but remote places.

Try listing some of the things you can do to add extra spice to life.

☐ Visit a new country
☐ Learn a new manual skill (embroidery, crochet, tatting, book-binding, car maintenance, carpentry)
☐ Take in a paying guest
☐ Join a local lunch club
☐ Start photography, film/video-making
☐ Take up painting, drawing, carving
☐ Sponsor an orphan in the Third World
☐ ....
☐ ....

We can bring into our lives special events, perhaps projects we could not consider when younger. Some things become easier when older. A voyage to the midnight sun may be more agreeable when we lead a largely sedentary existence than when we were energetic and found it difficult to sit still.

Write down a list of the holidays you would like to have had. Put them in order of possibility — could you still take one?

— London
— Blackpool
— Paris
— Pony trekking
— Coach tour to Austria
— Isles of Scilly
— Cross-Channel ferry to French port and hypermarket
— North America
— Cruise
— ....
— ....
— ....
— ....

Telephone and mail

The telephone can be a real window on the world whether one is housebound or not. We can receive calls from all over the world. And certainly within our own locality there will be plenty of people who would like to talk to us over the phone. We could even undertake voluntary (or paid) work that requires the use of the phone, perhaps as an answering service or in connection with an advice agency.

The mail can be an important link with the wider world, too, not just through personal correspondence, but in connection with some worthwhile cause in which we are interested. Addressing envelopes, writing or typing letters, dealing with enquiries, forwarding mail, writing off for information — these are some of the things that can help one become indispensable to voluntary agencies or mail order organisations.

Being useful

It's easy to forget that needing other people can almost be a service in itself. Most people have a great deal of love and affection in them and are only too willing to help someone else, especially when their help is not taken for granted. After all, all helpers need people to give their help to, and welcome an opportunity for their own personal fulfilment.

One of the rewards of helping is the response of the person helped. This does not have to be just saying thank you. We can offer kind words, conversation, a listening ear, small gifts and so on. If we show our appreciation in a simple way we are behaving no differently from a friend among friends. We offer friendship in return for friendship.

Two of the best qualities of older people are usually their **tolerance** and their **wisdom** (although it must be said that some old people can be bigoted and cantankerous). Tolerance and wisdom are qualities much yearned for by younger people as they go through the crises of their lives. Older people can show real sympathy and understanding and help far beyond what it costs by offering to listen to problems — especially those of a personal nature which may require long and patient attention — and can do this without being judgmental.

However old we are, we are still as important and useful as we have ever been. To understand this is the best basis for growing old gracefully.

Taking things easy

After a while we may for various reasons need to take things easier. Our morale may still be fine but physical energy and good health may be lacking and some things such as climbing stairs may cause distress. There are a number of things we can do to make life easier for us.

One of these is to go and live with relatives. One needs to make such a decision with the utmost care. Will there be enough room in the new home to give everyone the space they need? Will there be at least a comfortable room to retire to? Will there be access to outside if necessary? Old people can become distressed if they are cooped up in a flat after having a garden to walk out into.

All kinds of help can be obtained according to the needs of the elderly person and their hosts. **Day care** can be arranged through the local authority or daily help can be obtained privately. *Meals on wheels* can be organised for the house-ridden, and domestic help for those who cannot clean or look after themselves properly.

It is worth remembering that help is often available for those who have to look after a sick dependent. **Home responsibilities protection** is available for anyone who has to give up work to look after an elderly person. There is a **dependant relative's allowance** which is offset against tax for those contributing at least £75 a year towards the support of an elderly relative on the basic pension. And there is **invalid care allowance** for those who must stay at home to look after a parent.

There are also **attendance allowances** for those who are severely disabled, a **mobility allowance** for those who became unable to walk before the age of 65 and a **houskeeper's allowance** for a widow or widower who is forced to act as housekeeper (except for men in receipt of a married man's allowance). Details are available from local DHSS offices or local Citizens' Advice Bureaux. An excellent paperback guide is available from bookshops or public libraries, *How to Claim State Benefits* by Martin Rathfelder, published by Northcote House.

Sheltered housing

There is an increasing supply of sheltered housing both private and provided by the local authority or charities. Many have **wardens** in attendance, so that elderly people are always under someone's watchful eye. For many older people this provides a good transition from their own housing to either hospital, nursing home, retirement home or before going to live with a member of the family.

Many forms of special housing exist and it is a good idea to decide on the sort we feel will suit us best before the choice has to be made, and before someone else does it for us. In all probability the decision to provide special accommodation will be made by someone else, and perhaps in something of an emergency. We should remember that our family will probably have thought about this for some time before the subject is actually broached, and have reached some decisions to which we may not be an eager party. If we can make our *own* plans, we will probably be a lot more comfortable than if others decide what suits them.

Help available

A considerable amount of help is available in most areas from voluntary organisations, in addition to statutory Health and Social Security provision.

Such services are provided by the local Department of Health & Social Security, the British Red Cross Society, St John's Ambulance Brigade, Womens' Royal Voluntary Service, Help the Aged, and other agencies listed in the **Useful Addresses** section at the back of this book.

All in all a vast amount of help is available today for those who are in need. Even those without the health they would wish need not lack for comfort and companionship.

Help for the elderly

- ☐ day centres and clubs
- ☐ transport
- ☐ home visiting
- ☐ gardening
- ☐ odd jobbing
- ☐ lunch clubs and meals on wheels
- ☐ invalid aids
- ☐ collection of medical prescriptions
- ☐ family support
- ☐ holidays
- ☐ advice and information
- ☐ specialist care
- ☐ crisis support
- ☐ shopping outings
- ☐ day and night sitting
- ☐ provision of reading material (eg for blind, partially sighted but also the housebound)

Checklist
Growing Older

- ☐ Positive attitude despite minor ailments?
- ☐ More able to slow down and relax if necessary?
- ☐ Plenty of contact with family, friends and the community?
- ☐ Plenty of adventure and one or two real highlights in store?
- ☐ Making good use of the telephone and letter-writing?
- ☐ Being useful to others?
- ☐ Investigated help and services for the future — meals, housing, domestic help, transport?
- ☐ Claiming any benefits to which you are entitled from the Department of Health & Social Security?
- ☐ Checked the addresses/contacts at the back of this book?

Further Reading

Approaching Retirement (Consumer Association 1984)

Easing into Retirement, Keith Hughes (Legal & General Assurance Society 1985)

Finance, Douglas Shields (Charles Letts & Co 1985)

Gabbitas-Thring Guide to Independent Further Education, ed. Len Shaw (Northcote House Publishers 1987, 2nd edition)

The Good Health Guide, Open University (Harper & Row 1980)

The Good Retirement Guide, Rosemary Brown (Duckworth 1987)

House & Garden, Grace Shackleton (Charles Letts & Co 1986)

How to Claim State Benefits, Martin Rathfelder (Northcote House Publishers 1987)

How to Raise Business Finance, Peter Ibbetson (Northcote House Publishers 1987)

How to Use a Library, Elizabeth King (Northcote House Publishers 1987)

Leisure & Travel, Audrey Colville (Charles Letts & Co 1986)

Making the Most of Your Money, Louise Botting & Vincent Duggleby (Orbis 1984)

Money in the 1980s: How to Make It, How to Keep It, William Davis (Wiedenfeld & Nicholson 1981)

Planning for Retirement, Tom Levene (Daily Telegraph 1986)

Retiring Abroad?, Harry Brown (Northcote House Publishers 1987)

Successful Retirement, Roy Assersohn (Robert Boyce 1982)

What Will My Pension Be? (Consumer Association 1979)

Where to Live After Retirement (Consumer Association 1979)

Work After Work, Judy Kirby (Quiller Press 1986)

Working Abroad?, Harry Brown (Northcote House Publishers 1986)

Working at Home for Profit, Joanna Johnson (Basil Blackwell 1980)

Glossary

Annuity. A sum received each year. Usually these are Purchased Life Annuities whereby, in exchange for a lump sum, a life assurance company pays a regular pension for life. Since part of each payment is regarded as a repayment of capital, only the balance is subject to tax. It is possible to buy an annuity which increases annually by a fixed rate and/or which is guaranteed to be paid for a minimum period — usually five years. Whatever type is bought, the terms cannot be changed by the purchaser or the insurer afterwards.

Assurance. A form of saving linked to a future event such as retirement. Savings accumulate with interest until a certain age is reached or death intervenes.

Capital Gains Tax. A tax on the scale of certain goods and properties, usually excluding the home in which you live. Individuals are exempt from certain sums set by the Chancellor of the Exchequer, according to the Finance Act which follows the Budget each year.

Citizens' Advice Bureaux. Special bureaux which give advice on almost all matters but particularly government and official policy matters. Most towns have a Bureau which is staffed by voluntary but specially trained advisers. They can supply information about most current legislation.

Credit Transfer. You can use this to have your pension paid directly into a bank or Giro account. Payment will be made in arrears.

Earnings Rule. Those in receipt of retirement pension may only earn up to a certain sum (varying from time to time) before their pension becomes taxable. The earning rule does **not** apply after the age of 70.

Endowment Policy. A Life Insurance policy in which savings are made for a specified number of years. On maturity a lump sum is payable which may be reinvested in, for example, an annuity.

Financial Consultant. Anyone offering financial advice. May be independent or attached to an insurance company or investment corporation. Introductions best obtained through your bank.

Fixed Notice Shares. Building Society Shares which attract a slightly higher rate of interest, in return for the period of notice being longer than usual for withdrawal (generally three to nine months).

Gilt Edged Securities (Gilts). Government Stocks with guaranteed repayment price (at a future date) and fixed rate of interest. Can be bought through Post Offices and traded on the Stock Exchange (prices fluctuate). Stocks issued by the government are free of Capital Gains Tax if held for at least one year. They can be chosen for a required period and for a mix of income and capital growth.

Granny Bonds. SAYE with a maximum investment of £5,000. Period of 1 to 5 years. After a year the value is increased in line with inflation. After 5 years a bonus of 4% is payable.

Inheritance Tax. Government Tax on gifts made within 7 years of death (except between husband and wife). Applies to total value of estate over £90.000 (1987).

Insurance. Protection against some event that may or may not happen such as a burglary, road accident or fire. Premiums do not accrue or gain interest. The usual forms of insurance are House (Property) Insurance, House Contents Insurance, Car Insurance. Many people also take out Private Health Insurance and Holiday Insurance (often obligatory).

Insurance Broker. A registered professional who can give advice on all forms of financial investment including insurance, life policies and pensions. Must be a member of the British Insurance Brokers' Association.

Legal Aid. In some cases, individuals are entitled to financial support in legal disputes or claims. Full advice from your local Citizens Advice Bureau.

Local Authority Bonds. Offer a fixed rate of interest paid automatically each month. There are two types: Bonds which must remain invested for a fixed period, and Yearling Bonds which can be sold at any time on the Stock Exchange.

Mortgage Annuity. Method of paying for an annuity while paying off the mortgage on a house; effectively the house is used as security or collateral.

Nursing Home. Residential home with nursing attendance. Usually available only for elderly people requiring nursing attention but who are not acutely sick.

Pension. Any regular sum paid to a retired person. The State Pension is paid only to those of pensionable age but other forms of pension (eg company, army, police) are payable in addition.

Pensionable Age. For men the age is 65 and for women 60.

Pension Book. Book of coupons against which the State Pension is paid. Usually used to identify old age pensioners who may be entitled to other concessions, eg reduced fares on public transport.

Pension Fund. Fund from which a pension is paid. Company pension funds are separately managed from the company awarding the pension.

Personal Equity Plan. New scheme (1987) whereby a regular monthly sum of up to £200 a month can be invested on the Stock Exchange through an authorised manager. Provides regular dividends plus capital growth.

Residential Home. See **Rest Home.**

Rest Home. Provides residential accommodation for those who are not in very bad health. Usually rooms are shared, and fully qualified nursing staff may not be available.

Retirement Village. Housing designed specially for retired people and often with some special provision, though not the same as 'sheltered housing'.

Save As You Earn (SAYE). Regular monthly savings from income for a period of 5 years. At the end of the term a bonus is payable equal to 14 months savings. If left for a further two years the bonus is doubled.

Share Account. The normal form of account in a Building Society. Offers the lowest rate of interest, but withdrawal is on short notice or even on demand.

Sheltered Housing. Housing built specially for retired and older people either by a local authority or Housing Association, with a warden in regular attendance.

Subscription Shares. For regular monthly savings at a Building Society of sums from £1 to £100. Interest rate may vary but is normally guaranteed.

Taxation. State pensions are not taxed if they are sole income. If, however, there is another source of income, such as a private pension, the *whole* income, including the State Pension, is taxed in the normal way.

Term Shares. A sum invested in a Building Society for a fixed period of years; it attracts a higher rate of interest than ordinary shares.

Unit Trusts. Investment in stocks and shares by professional fund
managers. The yield will vary; and it is generally best used for capital
growth. Units can be bought and sold on the Stock Market.

Useful Addresses

Business and Finance

Association of Investment Trust Companies, 16 Finsbury Circus, London EC2.

Banking Information Service, 10 Lombard Street, London EC3V 9AT.

Barclays Bank plc, Juxon House, St Paul's Churchyard, London EC4M 8EH.

British Executives Overseas Service, 10 Belgrave Square, London SW1Y 8PH. Tel: (01) 235 1576.

British Insurance Association, Aldermary House, 10-15 Queen Street, London EC4N 1TU. Tel: (01) 248 4477.

British Insurance Brokers' Association, Biba House, 14 Bevis Marks, London EC3A 7NT. Tel: (01) 623 9043.

Career Analysts, Career House, 90 Gloucester Place, London W1. Tel: (01) 935 5452.

CEPEC (Centre for Professional Employment Counselling), 67 Jermyn Street, London SW1Y 6NZ. Tel: (01) 930 0322.

Chamber of Commerce. *See local telephone directory.*

Company Pensions Information Centre, Old Park Lane, London W1Y 3LJ. Tel: (01) 493 4757.

Corps of Commissionnaires, 3 Crane Court Street, London EC4 2EJ. Tel: (01) 353 2125. (Almost exclusively for those who have worked in uniformed services.)

COSIRA (Council for Small Industries in Rural Areas), 141 Castle Street, Salisbury, Wilts SP11 3TP. Tel: (0722) 336255.

Employment Fellowship, Wensley House, Bell Common, Epping, Essex CM16 4DY. Tel: (0378) 77047.

Executive Standby Ltd., Office 51, The London Wool & Fruit Exchange, Brushfield Street, London E1 6EU. Tel: (01) 247 5693. *Or* 310 Chester Road, Hartford, Northwich, Cheshire CW8 2AB. (Also in Bristol and Evesham.)

Gabbitas-Thring Educational Trust, 6 Sackville Street, London W1. Tel: (01) 734 0161. (Educational agency and contact for private coaching or teaching.)

Halifax Building Society, Head Office, PO Box 60, Trinity Road, Halifax, W. Yorks. Tel: (0422) 65777. (Range of services for older people.)

Institute of Chartered Accountants in England and Wales, PO Box 433, Chartered Accountants' Hall, Moorgate Place, London EC2P 2JK.

Institute of Chartered Accountants in Ireland, 87-89 Pembroke Road, Dublin 4, Eire.

Institute of Chartered Accountants in Scotland, 27 Queen Street, Edinburgh EH2 1LA.

Institute of Management Consultants, 23 Cromwell Place, London SW7 2LG. Tel: (01) 584 7285.

Insurance Brokers' Registration Council, 15 St Helen's Place, London EC3A 6DS.

The Law Society, 113 Chancery Lane, London WC2A 1PL. Tel: (01) 242 1222.

Legal Aid Head Office, Newspaper House, 8-16 New Street, London EC4N 3BN. Tel: (01) 353 7411.

Life Offices Association, Aldermary House, Queen Street, London EC4.

Lloyds Bank plc., 71 Lombard Street, London EC3P 3BS.

Manpower Ltd., Manpower House, 270-272 High Street, Slough, Bucks SL1 1LJ. Tel: (0753) 73311.

Market Research Society, 175 Oxford Street, London W1R 1TA. Tel: (01) 439 2585.

Midland Bank plc., Poultry, London EC2P 2BX.

National Advisory Centre on Careers for Women, Drayton House, 30 Gordon Street, London WC1H 0AX. Tel: (01) 380 0117.

National Association of Security Dealers & Investment Managers, 28 Lovat Lane, London EC3R 8EB.

National Association of Shopkeepers of Great Britain & Northern Ireland, Lynch House, 91 Mansfield Road, Nottingham.

National Federation of Self Employed & Small Business Ltd., 140 Lower Marsh, London SE1 7AE.

National Westminster Bank plc, 41 Lothbury, London EC2P 2BP.

Nationwide Building Society, Head Office, New Oxford House, High Holborn, London WC1V 6PW. Tel: (01) 242 8822.

Occupational Pensions Advisory Service, Room 327, Aviation House, 129 Kingsway, London WC2 6NN. Tel: (01) 405 6922 (Ext. 205).

Part-Time Careers Ltd., 10 Golden Square, London W1R 3AF. Tel: (01) 437 3103.

Prudential Assurance Company Ltd., 142 Holborn Bars, London EC1. Tel: (01) 405 9222.

Publishers' Association, 19 Bedford Square, London WC1. Tel: (01) 580 6321.

REACH (Retired Executives Action Clearing House), 89 Southwark Street, London SE1 0HD. Tel: (01) 928 0452.

Royal Bank of Scotland plc., 42 St Andrew Square, Edinburgh EH2 2YE.

Small Firms Information Service (Department of Trade & Industry). Tel: 100 — Freephone 2444.

Society of Pension Consultants, Ludgate House, Ludgate Circus, London EC4A 2AB. Tel: (01) 353 1688.

Stock Exchange, Public Affairs Department, London EC2N 1HP. Tel: (01) 588 2355. (Publish a booklet, *An Introduction to Buying & Selling Shares*).

Success After Sixty, 40-41 Old Bond Street, London W1X 3AF. Tel: (01) 629 0672.

Truman & Knightley Educational Trust, 78 Notting Hill Gate, London W11 3LJ. Tel: (01) 727 1242.

Health and Fitness

Alcohol Concern, 305 Gray's Inn Road, London WC1 8QF. Tel: (01) 833 3471.

Alzheimers Disease Society, Third Floor, Bank Buildings, Fulham Broadway, London SW6 1EP. Tel: (01) 381 3177. *Or* First Floor, Shandwick Place, Edinburgh EH2 4RT. Tel: (031) 225 1453.

Arthritis Care, 6 Grosvenor Crescent, London SW1X 7EH. Tel: (01) 235 0902.

ASH, 5-11 Mortimer Street, London W1N 7RH. (Campaigns against smoking.)

Back Pain Association, 31-33 Park Road, Teddington, Middx TW11 0AB. Tel: (01) 977 5474.

BACUP (British Association of Cancer United Patients), 121-123 Charterhouse Street, London EC1 6AA. Tel: (01) 608 1661.

British Acupuncture Association, 34 Alderney Street, London SW1V 4EU. Tel: (01) 834 1012.

British Association for the Hard of Hearing, 7-11 Armstrong Road, London W3 7JL. Tel: (01) 743 1110.

British Chiropractic Association, 5 First Avenue, Chelmsford, Essex CM11 1RX. Tel: (0245) 358487.

British Dental Health Association, 88 Gurnards Avenue, Fishmead, Milton Keynes MD6 2BL. Tel: (0908) 667063.

British Diabetic Association, 10 Queen Anne Street, London W1M 0BD. Tel: (01) 323 1531.

British Homeopathic Association, 27a Devonshire Street, London W1N
1RJ. Tel: (01) 935 2163.
British Hypnotherapy Association, 67 Upper Berkeley Street, London
W1H 7DH. Tel: (01) 732 4443.
British Tinnitus Association, 105 Gower Street, London WC1. Tel: (01)
387 8033.
BUPA, Provident House, Essex Street, London WC2R 3AX. Tel: (01)
353 5212.

Central Council of Physical Education (Movement & Dance Division),
Franers House, Franers Street, London SW1P 1DE.
Chest, Heart & Stroke Association, Tavistock House North, Tavistock
Square, London WC1H 9JE. Tel: (01) 387 3012.

Depressives Associated, PO Box 5, Castletown, Portland, Dorset DT5
1BQ.

General Council of Osteopaths, 1-4 Suffolk Street, London SW1Y 4HG.
Tel: (01) 839 2060.

Health Education Authority, 78 New Oxford Street, London WC1A 1AH.

Incorporated Society of Registered Naturopaths, 328 Harrogate Road,
Leeds LS17 6PE. Tel: (0532) 685992.

Keep Fit Association, 16 Upper Woburn Place, London WC1H 0TG. Tel:
(01) 387 4349.

Look After Yourself Project Centre, Christ Church College, Canterbury,
Kent CT1 1QU. Tel: (0227) 455564.

Mastectomy Association of Great Britain, 26 Harrison Street, Gray's Inn
Road, London WC1H 2JG. Tel: (01) 837 0908.
Migraine Trust, 45 Great Ormond Street, London WC1N 3HD. Tel: (01)
278 2676.
Multiple Sclerosis Society, 25 Effie Road, London SW6 1EE. Tel: (01)
381 4022.

Parkinson's Disease Society, 36 Portland Place, London W1N 3DG. Tel:
(01) 323 1174.
PPP (Private Patients Plan), PPP House, Upperton Road, Eastbourne,
E. Sussex BN21 1LH. Tel: (0323) 641155.

Relaxation for Living, 29 Burwood Park Road, Walton-on-Thames,
Surrey KT12 5LH.
Royal National Institute for the Blind, 224 Great Portland Street, London
W1N 6AA. Tel: (01) 388 1266.

Royal National Institute for the Deaf, 105 Gower Street, London WC1E 6AH. Tel: (01) 387 8033.

Sports Council, 16 Upper Woburn Place, London WC1H 0QP. (Regional offices are listed in your local telephone directories. For Greater London and the South East, tel: (01) 778 8600. Sports Council for Wales, tel: (0222) 397571. Sports Council for Northern Ireland, tel: (0232) 661222. Scottish Sports Council, tel: (031) 225 8411.)

Weight Watchers, 11 Fairacres, Dedworth Road, Windsor, Berks SL4 4UY. Tel: (0753) 856751.

Western Provident Association Ltd., Culver House, Culver Street, Bristol BS1 5JE. Tel: (0272) 273241.

Women's League of Health & Beauty, 18 Charing Cross Road, London WC2H 0HT. Tel: (01) 241 8456.

Yoga Biomedical Trust, PO Box 140, Cambridge CB2 2HP. Tel: (0223) 65771.

Yoga for Health Foundation, Icknell Bury, Northill, Nr Biggleswade, Beds. Tel: (076) 727 271.

Hobbies and Interests

Amateur Music Association, 43 Renshaw Street, Liverpool L1 2SF. Tel: (051) 709 6862.

British Association of Numismatic Societies, Department of Numismatics, Manchester Museum, The University, Oxford Road, Manchester.

British Beekeepers' Association, National Agricultural Centre, Stoneleigh, Coventry CV8 2LZ. Tel: (0203) 552404.

British Chess Federation, 9a Grand Parade, St Leonards on Sea, E. Sussex TN33 0DD. Tel: (0424) 442500.

British Federation of Film Societies, 81 Dean Street, London W1. Tel: (01) 437 4355.

British Theatre Association, 9 Fitzroy Square, London W1P 6AE. Tel: (01) 387 2666.

British Trust for Conservation Volunteers, St Mary's Street, Wallingford, Oxfordshire. Tel: (0491) 39766.

Centre for Alternative Technology, Machynlleth, Powys SY20 9AZ. Tel: (0654) 2400.

Civic Trust, 17 Carlton House Terrace, London SW1Y 5AW. Tel: (01) 930 0914.

College of Adult Education. (Address in local Telephone Directory or from Local Education Authority).

Cookery Centre, 43 Norwich Avenue West, Bournemouth, Dorset BH2 6AJ. Tel: (0202) 293321.

Council for the Accreditation of Correspondence Colleges, 27 Marylebone Road, London NW1 5JS. Tel: (01) 935 5391.

Council for the Protection of Rural England, 4 Hobart Place, London SW1. Tel: (01) 235 9481.

Crafts Council, 12 Waterloo Place, London SW1. Tel: (01) 930 4811.

Cyclists Touring Club, Cotterell House, 69 Meadrow, Godalming, Surrey GU7 3HS. Tel: (04868) 7217.

Deanhouse Ltd., Publishers, The Mews House, Court Walk, Betley, Nr Crewe, Cheshire CW3 9DP. Tel: (0270) 820053. (Advice on self-financed publishing.)

Denman College, Marcham, Abingdon, Oxfordshire OX13 6NW. Tel: (0865) 391219. (Residential adult education centre of the National Federation of Women's Institutes.)

Embroiderers' Guild, Apartment 41a, Hampton Court Palace, East Molesey, Surrey KT8 9AU. Tel: (01) 943 1229.

English Bridge Union, 15b High Street, Thame, Oxon OX9 2BH. Tel: (01) (08442) 2221.

English Folk Dance & Song Society, Cecil Sharp House, 2 Regent's Park Road, London NW1 7AY. Tel: (01) 485 2206.

English Gardening School, Chelsea Physic Garden, 66 Royal Hospital Road, London SW3 4HS. Tel: (01) 351 4347.

Gardens for the Disabled Trust & Garden Club, Little Dane, Biddenden, Ashford, Kent. Tel: (0580) 291214.

Historical Association, 59a Kennington Park Road, London SE11 4JH. Tel: (01) 735 3901.

Imperial Society of Teachers of Dancing, Euston Hall, Birkenhead Street, London WC1H 8BE.

Lancaster University Summer School, Department of Adult Education, The University, Bailrigg, Lancaster LA1 4YW. Tel: (0524) 65201.

Lee Abbey, Lynton, N. Devon EX35 6JJ. Tel: (0598) 52621. (Christian community welcoming visitors.)

Leisure Learning Ltd., Embassy Hotels, Station Street, Burton-on-Trent, Staffs DE14 1BS. Tel: (0283) 66587.

National Adult School Organisation, Norfolk House, Smallbrook, Queensway, Birmingham B5 4LJ. Tel: (021) 643 9297.

National Association of Choirs, 13 Stafford Close, Bulkington, Nuneaton CU12 9QX.

National Association of Flower Arranging Societies of Great Britain, 21a Denbigh Street, London SW1. Tel: (01) 828 5145.

National Association of Townswomen's Guilds, Chamber of Commerce House, 72 Harbourne Road, Edgaston, Birmingham B15 3EA.

National Association of Women's Clubs, 5 Vernon Rise, King's Cross Road, London WC1X 9EP.

National Extension College, 18 Brooklands Avenue, Cambridge CB2 2HN. Tel: (0223) 316644.

National Federation of Women's Institutes, 39 Eccleston Street, Victoria, London SW1W 9WY.

National Institute of Adult & Continuing Education, 19b De Montfort Street, Leicster LE1 7GE. Tel: (0533) 551451.

National Philatelic Society, Room 28, 27 King Street, London WC2 8JD. Tel: (01) 240 7349.

National Sailing Centre, Arctic Road, Cowes, Isle of Wight. Tel: (0983) 295938.

National Society of Allotment & Leisure Gardeners Ltd., 22 High Street, Flitwick, Beds. MK45 1DT. Tel: (0536) 66576.

National Trust, 36 Queen Anne's Gate, London SW1H 9AS. Tel: (01) 222 9251.

National Trust for Scotland, 5 Charlotte Square, Edinburgh EH2 4DU. Tel: (031) 226 5922.

Network Scotland Ltd., 74 Victoria Crescent, Glasgow G12 9JQ. Tel: (041) 357 1774. (Information about courses of all description.)

Open University, Student Enquiry Office, PO Box 71, Milton Keynes MK7 6AG. Tel: (0908) 74066.

Poetry Society, 21 Earls Court Square, London SW5 9DE. Tel: (01) 373 7861.

Ramblers' Association, 1-5 Wandsworth Road, London SW8 2LJ. Tel: (01) 582 6826/6878.

Royal Horticultural Society, Vincent Square, London SW1 2PE. Tel: (01) 834 4333.

Royal Photographic Society, The Octagon, Milsom Street, Bath, Avon. Tel: (0225) 62841.

Royal Scottish Country Dance Society, 12 Coates Crescent, Edinburgh EH3 7AF. Tel: (031) 225 3854.

Royal Society for the Protection of Birds, The Lodge, Sandy, Beds. Tel: (0767) 80551.

Royal Zoological Society, London Zoo, Regent's Park, London NW1 4RY. Tel: (01) 722 3333. *Or* Whipsnade Zoo, Dunstable, Beds. LU6 2LF. Tel: (0582) 872171.

Saltire Society, Saltire House, Atholl Crescent, Edinburgh EH3 8HA. Tel: (031) 228 6621. (The premier Scottish Association.)

Scottish Community Drama Association, Saltire House, 13 Atholl Crescent, Edinburgh EH3 8HA. Tel: (031) 229 7838.

Scottish Conservation Projects Trust, 70 Main Street, Doune, Perthshire, FK16 6BW. Tel: (0786) 841479.

Scrabble Club Coordinator, 42 Elthiron Road, London SW6 4BW. Tel: (01) 731 2633.

Summer Academy, School of Continuing Education, The University, Canterbury, Kent CT2 7NX. Tel: (0227) 470402. (For study holidays at the universities of Kent, Durham, Birmingham, Edinburgh, Liverpool, East Anglia (Norwich), Sheffield and Swansea.)

University of the Third Age, 6 Parkside Gardens, London SW19 5EY. Tel: (01) 660 5431.

Wine Mine Club, Vintner House, River Way, Harlow, Essex CM20 2EA. Tel: (0279) 416291.

Workers' Educational Association, Temple House, 9 Upper Berkeley Street, London W1H 0BY. Tel: (01) 402 5608.

Serving Others

British Executives Overseas Service. *See* Business and Finance section.

Catholic Marriage Advisory Council, Clitherow House, 15 Lansdowne Road, London W11 3AJ. Tel: (01) 727 0141.

Leonard Cheshire Foundation, Leonard Cheshire House, 26-29 Maunsel Street, London SW1P 2QN. Tel: (01) 828 1822.

Christian Aid, PO Box No. 1, London SW9 8BH. Tel: (01) 733 5500.

Conservative Central Office, 32 Smith Square, Westminster, London SW1. Tel: (01) 222 9000.

Cooperative Development Agency, Broadmead House, 21 Panton Street, London EC2A 4DR.

CRUSE, Cruse House, 126 Sheen Road, Richmond, Surrey TW9 1UR. Tel: (01) 940 4818/9047. (Practical help and counselling for widows and their families.)

Employment Fellowship. *See* Business and Finance section.

Executive Standby Ltd. *See* Business and Finance section.

Family Service Units, 207 Old Marylebone Road, London NW1 5QP. Tel: (01) 402 5175.

Pauline Hyde & Associates, 49-51 Bedford Row, London WC1V 6RL. (Specialists in employment for the retired.)

Imperial Cancer Research Fund, Lincoln's Inn Fields, PO Box 123, London WC2A 3PX. Tel: (01) 242 0200.

Labour Party Headquarters, 150 Walworth Road, London SE17. Tel: (01) 703 0833.

Liberal Party, 1 Whitehall Place, London SW1. Tel: (01) 839 4092.

MIND (National Association for Mental Health), 22 Harley Street, London W1N 2ED. Tel: (01) 637 0741.

NACRO (National Association for the Care and Resettlement of Offenders), 169 Clapham Road, London SW9 0PU. Tel: (01) 582 6500.

National Association of Leagues of Hospital Friends, 38 Ebury Street, London SW1W 0LU. Tel: (01) 730 0103.

National Association of Victims Support Schemes, 17a Electric Lane, London SW9 8LA. Tel: (01) 737 2091.

National Council for Voluntary Organisations, 26 Bedford Square, London WC1B 3HU. Tel: (01) 636 4066.

National Marriage Guidance Council, Herbert Gray College, Little Church Street, Rugby, Warwicks CV21 3AP. Tel: (0788) 73241.

OXFAM, Oxfam House, 274 Banbury Road, Oxford OX2 7DZ. Tel: (0865) 56777.

REACH (Retired Executives Action Clearing House). *See* Business and Finance section.

Sue Ryder Foundation, Sue Ryder House, Cavendish, Suffolk CO10 8AY. Tel: (0787) 280252.

Samaritans, 17 Uxbridge Road, Slough, Berks SL1 1SN. Tel: (0753) 32713.

Social Democratic Party, 4 Cowley Street, London SW1. Tel: (01) 222 7999.

Soldiers, Sailors & Airmen's Families Association, 16-18 Old Queen Street, London SW1H 9HP. Tel: (01) 222 9221.

Success After Sixty. *See* Business and Finance section.

Voluntary Service Overseas, 9 Belgrave Square, London SW1X 8PW. Tel: (01) 235 5191.

The Volunteer Centre, 29 Lower King's Road, Berkhamsted, Herts. Tel: (04427) 73311.

Women's Royal Voluntary Service, 17 Old Park Lane, London W1Y 4AJ. Tel: (01) 499 6040.

Travel and Holidays

Air Travel Advisory Board. Tel: (01) 636 5000 or Tel: (01) 832 2000. (Advises on low cost fares to all parts of the world.)

Association for Promoting Retreats, Church House, Newton Road, London W2. Tel: (01) 727 7924.

British Airways, PO Box 10, Heathrow Airport, Hounslow, Middx. TW6 2JA.

British Insitute in Florence, Palazzo Lanfredini, Lungarno Guicciardina 9, Florence, Italy.

British Rail Travel. *See* local telephone directory or local travel agent.

British Universities Accommodation Consortium, General Office, University Park, Nottingham NG7 1BR. Tel: (0602) 504571.

Camping and Caravanning Club, 11 Lower Grosvenor Place, London SW1. Tel: (01) 828 1012.

Countrywide Holidays Association, Birch Heys, Cromwell Range, Manchester M14 6HU. Tel: (061) 225 1000.

Cox & King's Special Interest Holidays, 46 Marshall Street, London W1V 2PA. Tel: (01) 734 8291.

Department of Health & Social Security, Overseas Office, Newcastle Central Office, Longbenton, Newcastle-upon-Tyne NE98 1YX.

En Famille Agency (Overseas), Westbury House, Queen's Lane, Arundel, W. Sussex BN18 9JN.

Estudio General Luliano, c/o 24 High Street, Portsmouth PO1 2LS. Tel: (0705) 824095. (Runs courses in Spanish in Majorca.)

Eurocentres, 36 Honor Oak Road, London SE2 3SN. Tel: (01) 699 1174.

Farm Holidays Bureau, National Agricultural Centre, Stoneleigh, Kenilworth, Warwicks CV8 2LL. Tel: (0203) 555100.

Field Studies Council, Preston Montford, Montford Bridge, Shrewsbury SY4 1HW. Tel: (0743) 850674.

Flatford Mill Centre, East Bergholt, Nr Colchester, Suffolk CO7 6UI. Tel: (0206) 298283. (For field studies overseas.)

Frames National, 97 Southampton Row, London WC1B 4BQ. Tel: (01) 637 4171. (Coach tours in Britain and Europe.)

Goethe Institut, Zentralverwaltung, Rererat 31, Len Bach Platz 3, D-8000, Munchen, Federal Republic of Germany. *Or* Goethe Institute, 50 Princes Gate, Exhibition Road, London SW7 2PH. Tel: (01) 581 3344.

Golden Circle Holidays (Global Holidays), 200 Tottenham Court Road, London W1P 0JP. Tel: (01) 323 3266.

Golden Days (Intasun), Intasun House, Cromwell Avenue, Bromley, Kent BR2 9AQ. Tel: (01) 290 1900.

Golden Rail Holidays, PO Box 12, York YO1 1YK. Tel: (0904) 28992.

Gray Dawes Travel Ltd., 3 Cathedral Place, London EC4M 7DT. Tel: (01) 248 6474. (For travel on cargo vessels.)

Higher Education Accommodation Bureau, 36 Collegiate Crescent, Sheffield S10 2BP. Tel: (0704) 683759. (Accommodation at over 50 colleges and polytechnics.)

Highland Guides, Iverdruie, Aviemore, Inverness-shire PH22 1QH. Tel: (0479) 810729. (Retirement interest holidays in the Cairngorms.)

Holiday Care Service, 2 Old Bank Chambers, Station Road, Horley, Surrey RH6 9HW. Tel: (02934) 744535.

Holimarine, 171 Ivy House Lane, Bilston, W. Midlands WV14 9LD. Tel: (09073) 77235. (Self-catering holidays for the over-fifties.)

Home Interchange, 8 Hillside, Farningham, Kent DA4 0DD. Tel: (0322) 864527.

Homesitters, Moat Farm, Buckland, Aylesbury, Bucks HP22 5HY. Tel: (0296) 631289.

Horizon Holidays, Broadway, Edgbaston, Birmingham B15 1BB. Tel: (021) 643 2727.

International Friendship League, 4 Wilton Close, Taunton, Somerset TA1 4EZ. (Promotes international goodwill through travel, social contact and correspondence.)

Landmark Trust, Shottsbroke, Maidenhead, Berks. Tel: (0628) 825925. (Homes to rent of architectural merit or curiosity.)

National Express, 13 Regent Street, London SW1Y 4LR. (National bus and coach services.)

Pensioners Link, 19 Balfe Street, London N1 9EB. Tel: (01) 278 5501.

P & O Cruises, Beaufort House, St Botolph Street, London EC3A 7DX. Tel: (01) 283 8080.

Railway Correspondence & Travel Society, 20 Baker Street, York YO3 7AX. Tel: (0904) 642155. (Organises special rail trips at home and overseas.)

Ramblers' Holidays Ltd., 13 Longcroft House, Fretherne Road, Welwyn Garden City, Herts. AL8 4PQ.

Royal Viking Line, 3 Vere Street, London W1M 9HQ. Tel: (01) 734 0774.

Saga Holidays plc., Saga House, Enbrook House, Sandgate Hill, Folkestone, Kent CT20 3SG. Tel: (0303) 30030.

Scottish Farmhouse Holidays, Drumtenant, Ladybank, Fife KY7 7UG. Tel: (0337) 30451.

Scottish Field Studies Association, Kindrogan Field Centre, Enochdhu, Blairgowrie, Perthshire PH10 7PG. Tel: (0250) 81286.

Scottish Youth Hostels Association, 7 Glebe Crescent, Stirling Central FK8 2JA. Tel: (0786) 72821.

Thomson Holidays Ltd., Greater London House, Hampstead Road, London NW1 7SD. Tel: (01) 237 9321.

Trailfinders Travel Centre, 42-48 Earls Court Road, London W8. Tel: (01) 937 9631. (Bespoke holidays.)

Travelscene Ltd., 94 Baker Street, London W1. Tel: (01) 486 6411. (Special holidays for the over-fifties.)

Universal Aunts, 250 Kings Road, London SW3 5UE. Tel: (01) 351 5767. (Provides, and recruits for, home sitting service.)

Vacances en Campagne, Bignor, Nr Pulborough, W. Sussex RH20 1QD. Tel: (07987) 366. (Properties in rural areas of France.)

WEXAS, 45 Brompton Road, London SW3. Tel: (01) 589 0500. (Comprehensive travel service at bargain prices for independent travel.)

Worldwide Home Exchange Club, 45 Hans Place, London SW1X 0JZ. Tel: (01) 589 6055.

Youth Hostels Association, Trevelyan House, St Stephen's Hall, St Albans, Herts. Tel: (0727) 55251.

Welfare Organisations

Abbeyfield Society, 186-192 Darkes Lane, Potters Bar, Herts EN6 1AB Tel: (0707) 44845. (Sheltered housing schemes and aid for the aged.)

Age Concern (England), Bernard Sunley House, 60 Pitcairn Road, Mitcham, Surrey CR4 3LL. Tel: (01) 640 5431.

Age Concern (Northern Ireland), 128 Great Victoria Street, Belfast 2. Tel: (0232) 245729.

Age Concern (Scotland), 33 Castle Street, Edinburgh. Tel: (031) 225 5000.

Age Concern (Wales), 1 Park Grove, Cardiff. Tel: (0222) 371566/371821.

British Red Cross Society, 9 Grosvenor Crescent, London SW1X 7EJ. Tel: (01) 235 5454.

Catholic Housing Aid Society, 189a Old Brompton Road, London SW5 0AR. Tel: (01) 373 4961. (Housing advice on all matters to all enquirers.)

Central Council for Jewish Social Services, 212 Golders Green Road, London NW11 9DW. Tel: (01) 458 3282.

Counsel & Care for the Elderly, 131 Middlesex Street, London E1 7JF. Tel: (01) 621 1624.

Department of Health & Social Security (England), Alexander Fleming House, Elephant & Castle, London SE1 6BY.

Department of Health & Social Security (Scotland), 3 Lady Lawson Street, Edinburgh EH3 9SH.

Department of Health & Social Security (Wales), Government Buildings, Gabalfu, Cardiff CF4 4YJ.

Disabled Living Foundation, 380-384 Harrow Road, London W9 2HU. Tel: (01) 289 6111.

Distressed Gentlefolk's Aid Society, Vicarage Gate House, Vicarage Gate, London W1M 6HY. Tel: (01) 229 9341.

Elderly Accommodation Council, 1 Burward House, 31 Kensington Court, London W8. Tel: (01) 937 8700.

John Groom's Association for the Disabled, 10 Gloucester Drive, London N4 2LP. Tel: (01) 802 7272.

Help the Aged, St James's Walk, Farringdon, London EC1R 0BE. Tel: (01) 253 0253.

Housing Corporation, 149 Tottenham Court Road, London W1P 0BN. Tel: (01) 387 9466.

National Benevolent Fund for the Aged, 35 New Broad Street, London EC2. Tel: (01) 638 2281.

Shelter, 157 Waterloo Road, London SE1 8XF. Tel: (01) 633 9377.

St John Ambulance Brigade, 1 Grosvenor Crescent, London SW1X 7EF. Tel: (01) 235 5231.

Women's Royal Voluntary Service. *See* Serving Others section.

Miscellaneous

Building Centre, 26 Store Street, London WC1E 7BT. Tel: (01) 637 1022.

Building Employers' Federation, 82 New Cavendish Street, London W1M 8AD. Tel: (01) 580 5588.

Choice Publications Ltd., 12 Bedford Row, London WC1R 4DV. Tel: (01) 404 4320. (For information about courses run by the Pre-Retirement Association.)

Consumers' Association, Castlemead, Gascoyne Way, Hertford SG14 1LH. (*Which?* publications.)

DPS Consultants Ltd., 27 Preston Street, Faversham, Kent CT20 3SG. Tel: (0795) 531472. (Pre-retirement courses for senior executives.)

Electricity Consumers' Council, Brook House, 2-16 Torrington Place, London WC1E 7LL. Tel: (01) 636 5703.

Energy Efficiency Office, Room 1312, Thames House South, London SW1 4AJ.

Energy Projects Office, 2-4 Bigg Market, Newcastle-upon-Tyne NE1 1UT. Tel: (0632) 615677.

Federation of Master Builders, 33 John Street, London WC1N 2BB. Tel: (01) 242 7583.

Federation of Private Residents' Associations, 11 Dartmouth Street, London SW1H 9BL. Tel: (01) 222 0037.

Gas Consumers' Council, 4th Floor, 162 Regent Street, London W1R 5TB. Tel: (01) 439 0012.

Homecraft of London, 27 Trinity Road, London SW17 7SF. Tel: (01) 672 7070. (Sells practical equipment for the elderly and disabled.)

Institute of Plumbing, 64 Station Lane, North Street, Hornchurch, Essex RM12 6NB. Tel: (04024) 72791.

Legal & General Retirement Counselling Service, Legal & General Assurance Society Ltd., Kingswood House, Kingswood, Tadworth, Surrey KT20 6EU. Tel: (07373) 53456.

National Association of Almshouses, Billingbear Lodge, Wokingham, Berks RG11 5RU. Tel: (0344) 52922.

National Association of Citizens' Advice Bureaux, 115-123 Pentonville Road, London N1 9LZ.

National Association for Widows, c/o Stafford District Voluntary Services Centre, Chell Road, Stafford ST16 2QA.

National Federation of Old Age Pensions Associations, Melling House, 91 Preston New Road, Blackburn, Lancs. Tel: (0254) 52606.

Nationwide Housing Trust Ltd., 57 George Street, Altrincham, Cheshire WA14 1RJ. Tel: (061) 941 6245.

Northern Ireland Association of Citizens' Advice Bureaux, 211 Antrim Road, Belfast, Co Antrim BT15 2GN.

Northern Ireland Committee, National Federation of Housing Associations, 123 York Street, Belfast BT15 1AB. Tel: (0132) 30446.

Pensioners Link. *See* Travel and Holidays section.

Pre-Retirement Association of Great Britain & Northern Ireland, 19 Undine Street, Tooting, London SW17 8PP. Tel: (01) 767 3225/3226/3854.

Registered Nursing Homes Association, 75 Portland Place, London W1N 4AN. Tel: (01) 631 1524.

Retirement Housing (Saga Holidays), PO Box 65, Folkestone, Kent CT20 3SG. (Has a register of purpose-built retirement housing.)

Retirement Information Bureau, 12 Bedford Row, London WC1R 4DU.

Royal Institute of British Architects, 66 Portland Place, London W1N 4AB. Tel: (01) 580 5533.

Royal Institute of Chartered Surveyors, 12 Great George Street, Parliament Square, London SW1P 3AD. Tel: (01) 222 7000.

Scottish Association of Citizens' Advice Bureaux, 82 Nicholson Street, Edinburgh EH8 9EW.

Scottish Federation of Housing Associations Ltd., 42 York Place, Edinburgh EH1 3HU. Tel: (031) 556 1435.

Scottish Old Age Pensions Association, 3 Boswell Place, Edinburgh EH5 0BT. Tel: (031) 552 4627.

Index

How To . . . Books
Opening Doors of Opportunity

A major series of self-help paperbacks packed with valuable information on new opportunities in today's fast-changing world. Each of these user-friendly handbooks gives clear up-to-date information and advice, prepared by experts, and complete with checklists for action and self-assessment material. The guides will save you time and money by supplying essential information which is often hard to find.

Helpfully clear layout with illustrations and cartoons, glossary, useful sources, index. Each 215 x 135mm, £3.95 approx.

You can't afford to miss the 'How To . . . series'

How to Pass Exams Without Anxiety David Acres
A step by step guide to removing stress and achieving success in exams at every level.
0 7463 0334 3

How to Raise Business Finance Peter Ibbetson
A down-to-earth guide for the self-employed and small business needing financial assistance.
0 7463 0338 6

How to Live and Work in Australia Laura Veltman
The unique handbook for all those considering employment and residence 'Down Under'.
0 7463 0331 9

How to Live and Work in America Steve Mills
Packed with new ideas on home life, leisure, travel, social and business opportunities.
0 7463 0323 8

How to Help Your Child at School John West-Burnham
Vital information and advice for every concerned parent.
0 7463 0329 7

How to Use a Library Elizabeth King
A fascinating guide to the many opportunities offered by libraries today for study, work and leisure.
0 7463 0317 3

How to Claim State Benefits Martin Rathfelder
Making sense of the system.
0 7463 0505 2

Dozens more titles in preparation. For details please contact Dept BPA.
Northcote House Publishers Ltd., Harper & Row House,
Estover Road, Plymouth PL6 7PZ, United Kingdom.
Tel: Plymouth (0752) 705251 Telex: 45635.